# THE ANOINTED LIFE

*To: Megan*
*Walk in your Anoint[ing]*
*Love, Carol[yn]*

# THE ANOINTED LIFE

## CRUCIFYING THE FLESH

## CAROLYN CHAMBERS

ANOINTED LIFE PUBLISHING COMPANY
Phoenix, Arizona

THE ANOINTED LIFE
Crucifying the Flesh

Printed in the United States of America
Library of Congress Cataloging-In-Publication Data
Chambers, Carolyn
The Anointed Life / Carolyn Chambers
p. cm Library of Congress Control Number: 1-1304706531

ISBN:      Hardcover        978-0-9906465-2-5
ISBN:      Softcover        978-0-615-99362-1
ISBN:      Ebook            970-0-9906465-3-2

1. Ministry
2. Religion
3. Self Help

Editing and book design by Keith H. Chambers
Cover Design by C W Technology Consulting

www.anointedlifepublishing.com

# *Dedication*

This book is dedicated to the following:

- My father, Claude Sr., who endeavored to give each of us unconditional love. He taught me the value of showing your heart. While pouting, because I thought we could not afford a graduation dress for me, he said, "If I could, I would buy you a thousand dresses." Although he sacrificed and bought me a beautiful dress, it was seeing his heart that blessed me the most. His words continue to warm my heart, even now.

- My mother, Ruth, who in wielding her wisdom as a double-edged sword, taught me to envy her relationship with God. How blessed we were to sit daily under her wisdom!

- Special thanks to the Holy Spirit who gave me the confidence and anointing to pen this book. Thank God for the Holy Spirit!

# Contents

*Dedication* .................................................................................v

*Preface*.................................................................................. ix

*Acknowledgments* ........................................................... xi

*Introduction*.................................................................. xiii

Chapter 1 Life in the Flesh...............................................1

    Gedaliah's Errors of Commission...............................5

    Gedaliah's Errors of Omission...................................13

Chapter 2  Ten Men.........................................................35

Chapter 3 The Crucified Life...........................................41

Chapter 4  The Fruit of the Spirit...................................73

Chapter 5  Prescriptions for Life....................................87

Chapter 6  The Anointed Life.......................................129

Epilogue.........................................................................160

Appendix A Types of Flesh in the Bible.......................161

Appendix B Confessions................................................165

# *Preface*

Years ago, a woman, along with her two children, visited my church. Grieving, she requested to share a personal story with the congregation. She then went on to recount the events surrounding the death of her husband.

She and her husband had made plans to take a vacation. Shortly thereafter, they heard that her father had taken ill. She thought that they should postpone the vacation and visit her dad, but the husband felt that it was a long awaited and much needed vacation; that it was best to keep their plans and visit her dad afterwards.

While on vacation, he decided to go surfing. She sensed the need to wait, but the husband felt that there was no time like the present. So, he took the two kids with him while she stayed behind at the hotel. Tragically, while surfing, the husband was overcome by high waves and drowned, but the two kids were rescued.

Overwhelmed by the story, I asked God, "What happened?" He said, "The flesh killed him." Alarmed and shaken, I needed to know more about the flesh. My interest turned into years of Bible research, and this book is a result of my endeavors.

The flesh is known as the fallen nature; it is hostile toward God. It is known as the enemy of the spirit man. It houses thoughts that are contrary to the will of God and actively fights against our soul: will, mind, emotions, intellect, and imagination. Although it wages a battle of thoughts for the control of the soul, its tactics are innocently perceived as just another idea, or another choice. In essence, it conducts a type of civil war battle that you fight with yourself, daily. This book is a call to win that battle.

For those of us who have fallen behind enemy lines, there is a way of escape, and it is through the fruit of the Spirit. This book exposes the flesh's need for affections and lusts (influence and the forbidden). It will empower the reader to even the playing field, knowing that when we fight the thoughts, we automatically win.

The Anointed Life takes you through the maturation process of the Christian life: from living life by prescription (salvation of the soul), to the crucified life (fruit of the Spirit), to the anointed life (lived freely under the influence of the Holy Spirit). It will challenge you to examine the foundation of your thoughts, beliefs, and convictions.

## *Acknowledgments*

Special thanks to my multi-talented husband, Keith, for his devotion to excellence. Having found your place, you make it an Eden and the people of God heirs. You find your sufficiency in the grace of God.

Thanks to my boys, Nehemiah and Zacharias, for the sacrifices that you made while I focused on my writing and research. Thank you for aligning your agendas to mine. You both have grown up in your youth.

*AND THEY BEND THEIR TONGUES*

*LIKE THEIR BOWS FOR LIES*

*BUT THEY ARE NOT VALIANT FOR THE TRUTH*

*UPON THE EARTH;*

*THEY PROCEED FROM EVIL TO EVIL,*

*AND THEY KNOW NOT ME, SAITH THE LORD*

JEREMIAH 9:3

## *Introduction*

The tests of life come to us all. But what would cause some people to pass life's tests while others fail?

The Anointed Life identifies a man, in the book of Jeremiah, by the name of Gedaliah, who refused wisdom and instead chose to follow his flesh; with devastating consequences for himself and perils for others. This book will take you through the numerous fateful errors that Gedaliah made as we examine the many devices that the flesh uses to deceive us. We will see what he did, learn the whys and hows of his actions, and analyze his behavior in the light of the progressive revelations laid out in the New Testament.

By contrast, we will look at a group of people who could have suffered the same fate as Gedaliah, but who rose above the situation. Their parable is a lesson on the power of faith: being a hearer and a doer of the word.

The Anointed Life asserts that the <u>flesh</u>, not the tests of life, is the real enemy of our soul. The Bible gives numerous examples of its potential influence on virtually every aspect of our lives, and it also gives us the defining tools to ultimately defeat this enemy.

The Fruit of the Spirit equips us to crucify the flesh and inherit the kingdom of God. It enables us to *heap coals of fire* on the unrighteous nature of an unlovely individual while sparing and empowering their righteous nature. We are not moved by the afflictions of life; we are settled. The Anointed Life references scriptures that detail <u>what</u> each fruit is, <u>why</u> it should be utilized, and <u>how</u> to use it.

Prescriptions for Life address the needs of the soul. After salvation, all the enemies have not been expelled off our land. Our spirits have been saved, but our souls have no rest. The soul consist of the mind, the will, the emotions, the intellect, and the imagination. Only the engrafted word of God can save our souls. Each prescription gives detailed guidance on how to expel the inhabitants from your spiritual land.

Finally, you will gain insight and instruction regarding <u>living</u> the Anointed Life, that is, a life that is lived *freely* under the influence of the Holy Spirit. It is the final stage of Christian development, it is the spiritual man taking its ascendency over the flesh and the natural man; operating through a renewed mind and the fruit of the Spirit. These are the anointed. Those who live the anointed life, through the guidance of the Holy Spirit, are assigned as ambassadors to bring comfort to the afflicted by reconciling God's people to Himself.

This book gives us a glimpse of life in the spirit: the predestined work and the prepared path that enables us to live the prearranged good life. Living under a better covenant, we have the opportunity to use Gedaliah's errors to our benefit and change the trajectory of our lives.

# Chapter 1

## Life in the Flesh

### Gedaliah Speaks Falsehood

In the book of Jeremiah, chapter 40, the king of Babylon took most of the people of Jerusalem and Judah captive to Babylon. He left a remnant of them not carried away captive (men, women, and children of the poor of the land), and made Gedaliah governor over them.

A group of men, led by Johanan (a captain of the forces that were in the fields) heard of a plot by a man named Ishmael, to kill Gedaliah. Afraid that the remnant might be scattered, Johanan and others came to Gedaliah and informed him of the secret plot. The Bible says that Gedaliah *believed them not*. Being certain that the plot was real, Johanan came a second time, desperately urging Gedaliah to defend himself, saying: *"Let me go, I pray thee, and I will slay Ishmael the son of Nethaniah, and no man shall know it: wherefore should he slay thee, that all the Jews which are gathered unto thee should be scattered, and the remnant in Judah perish,"* (Jeremiah 40:15). But Gedaliah adamantly asserted that Johanan was lying on Ishmael, stating: *"Thou shalt not do this thing: for thou speakest falsely of Ishmael,"* (Jeremiah 40:16).

One chapter later, the Bible says that Ishmael, along with ten other men, came and ate bread with Gedaliah. Afterwards, Ishmael arose and killed Gedaliah and the other Jews that were with him (see Jeremiah 41).

In John 8:32, Jesus preached that: *"And ye shall know the truth, and the truth shall make you free."* This story caught my attention because truth failed. In researching what would cause truth to fail, the prophet Isaiah explains the cause of such failure and how it affects the heart of the Father. He says truth fails when we: *"Conceive and utter from the heart words of falsehood,"* (Isaiah 59:13).

The problem began when Gedaliah spoke falsehood from his heart. He called Johanan a liar, saying: *"Thou speaketh falsely of Ishmael."* Verses 14-15 of Isaiah 59, points out what happens when we deceive ourselves, by conceiving and speaking falsehood (lies) from the heart; a series of reactions occur: *"Judgment is turned away backward, Justice stands afar off: for truth is fallen in the street and, Equity cannot enter. Yea, truth faileth; and he that departeth from evil maketh himself a prey: And the Lord saw it and it displeased Him that there was no judgment."*

The Lord is displeased when there is no judgment against deception. Why? Because:

- When truth fails, we cannot be set free—we become a prey.
- When equity cannot enter—we cannot turn from our iniquity.
- When justice stands afar off—we cannot be justified by faith.
- When judgment is turned away backward—we will now serve our enemy.

This is the devastation that occurs when an individual conceives and speaks falsehood from his heart; when he allows himself to be deceived.

Decisions that are made from the heart, whether they are right or wrong, govern our lives. They will justify us, or condemn us. And, because words spoken by our mouths come from our hearts, we are subject to them. Our hearts depend on us to examine our own thoughts

2

(before receiving them), to guard against falsehood. Gedaliah failed to judge his thoughts of unbelief, and his unbelief eventually killed him. Unbelief can be defined as believing something God did not say. It is normally prevalent where the will of God is not known, and it seems to affect even the best of us.

Consider King David, who had it in his heart to build a house for the Lord: *"And the Lord said unto David my father, Whereas it was in thine heart to build an house unto my name, thou didst well in that it was in thine heart: notwithstanding thou shalt not build the house; but thy son which shall come forth out of thy loins he shall build the house for my name,"* (1 Kings 8:18-19).

We have all been taught to follow our hearts, especially in areas of wanting to do a good deed. Here, God is telling David, it was a nice thought, but your heart is deceiving you. Your son, Solomon, will build my house. The message is: you can't trust your heart to guide you. Why? Because Jeremiah 17:9 says: *"The heart is deceitful above all things, and desperately wicked: who can know it?"* This precept is further established in Proverbs 28:26 that says: *"He that trusteth in his own heart is a fool: but whoso walketh wisely, he shall be delivered."* Gedaliah's only duty was to believe. Instead, he withstood the counsel of Johanan.

When the Virgin Mary believed the angel Gabriel, Elizabeth told her: *"And blessed is she that believed: for there shall be a performance of those things told her from the Lord,"* (Luke 1:45). God says that when you believe, more will be given to you: *"For unto everyone that has shall be given, and he shall have abundance: but from him that has not shall be taken away even that which he has,"* (Matthew 25:29).

Words of faith are not validated in the natural. The Bible says, Abraham went not knowing. Gedaliah rejected the words of truth but failed to hold his own thoughts of unbelief to the same scrutiny. He had no problem receiving unbelief from his own heart, but he held the truth, suspect. He trusted himself.

3

It takes faith to believe, but faith is not blind. It requires the process of consideration.

The Bible, in Proverbs 23:1, earnestly commands us saying: *"Consider diligently what is before us, when we sit down to eat with a ruler: put a knife to our throat if we be a man given to appetite."* This admonition requires us to consider diligently what thoughts we are receiving: *"For as he thinketh in his heart so is he,"* (Proverbs 23:7).

Proverbs is telling us that thoughts enter into our hearts, and wrong thoughts can defile it; because you become the thoughts that you receive. If the thought tells you to steal and you are caught stealing…we call you a thief. If you are tempted to lie and you do…we call you a liar. Thoughts from our hearts should produce life. Gedaliah's thoughts produced an evil heart of unbelief. In obeying his own heart, he was deceived.

God says in Isaiah 1:3: *"The ox knoweth his owner, and the ass his master's crib: but Israel doth not know, my people doth not consider."* We are commanded to consider our ways: *"There is a way which seemeth right unto a man, but the end thereof are the ways of death,"* (Proverbs 14:12). Gedaliah failed to consider that his way of thinking could lead to his death.

## Gedaliah's Errors of Commission

In analyzing Gedaliah's errors in judgment, some were <u>errors of commission</u> (things he did wrong). These were the mistakes that were made from his head. They will be examined using a format of biblical: wisdom (What), understanding (Why), and knowledge (How).

### Gedaliah Trusted In His Own Heart

**What:** *"Trust in the LORD with all thine heart;*
**Why:** *and lean not unto thine own understanding.*
**How:** *In all thy ways acknowledge him, and he shall direct thy paths,"* (Proverbs 3:5-6).

**Gedaliah's error**: He leaned to his own understanding: *"O Lord, I know that the way of man is not in himself: it is not in man that walketh to direct his steps,"* (Jeremiah 10:23).

**The right path**: When we acknowledge Him: *The words of His lips keep us from the paths of the destroyer; He leads us in paths of righteousness for his Name sake; He will lead us in a plain path, because of our enemies; Cause us to ponder path of our feet, and let all our ways be established.*

**The defeat of the flesh**: I had been working with my niece, who is normally headstrong, on watching the thoughts from her heart. Shortly thereafter, she applied for a dorm room for the summer. She was told that the registration period had ended. She then decided to take the matter to the dean, who began echoing the same sentiment. Her flesh told her that the dean was picking on her, because she was a minority. It advised her to curse him out. Instead of receiving that thought, she spoke softly to herself saying, "No, I can't say that, give me something else to say." Her spirit then spoke up and gave her the wisdom for the situation. After speaking kindly to the dean, he made an exception and honored her request.

**Commentary**: To understand is to acknowledge His paths for our lives.

5

## Gedaliah was Immature

**What:** *"Woe to thee, O land,*
**Why:** *When thy king is a child, and thy princes eat in the morning!*
**How:** *Blessed art thou, O land, when thy king is the son of nobles, and thy princes eat in due season, for strength, and not for drunkenness,"*
(Ecclesiastes 10:16-17).


**Gedaliah's error**: He was childish.
**The right path:** *The heir, as long as he is a child, differs nothing from a servant, though he be lord of all; That we henceforth be no more children, tossed to and fro, and carried about with every wind of doctrine, by the sleight of men, and cunning craftiness, whereby they lie in wait to deceive; Let no man deceive you with vain words: for because of these things cometh the wrath of God upon the children of disobedience; As obedient children, not fashioning yourselves according to your former lusts in your ignorance; walk as children of light.*
**The defeat of the flesh:** A man was kept in an impotent state for thirty-eight years, believing that he needed help to get into the pool at Bethesda to receive healing. Jesus passed by the man and asked him if he would be made whole. The man recited his 'song' of how he had no man to help him into the pool. Jesus didn't say, your mind is right, let me help you get into the pool. Instead, Jesus said: *"Rise, take up your bed and walk,"* (John 5:5-8). The Bible said: *"The man took up his bed and walked."* He never needed the pool: he only needed edifying. His mind deceived him, robbed him of his inheritance, and robbed him of his self-esteem for thirty-eight years.

A childish king (one who does not challenge his thoughts) differs nothing from a slave, thou he is lord of all. Maturity is not an option for the child of God, it is a necessity!
**Commentary:** Childish kings do not eat in due season—their enemies do.

## Gedaliah was in Love with Himself

**What:** *"In the last days, perilous times shall come*
**Why:** <u>*For men shall be lovers of their own selves*</u>*, covetous, boasters, proud, blasphemers, disobedient to parents, unthankful, unholy, without natural affection, trucebreakers,* <u>*false accusers*</u>*, incontinent, fierce,* <u>*despisers of those that are good*</u>*, Traitors, heady, high minded, lovers of pleasures more than lovers of God; Having a form of Godliness, but denying the power thereof:*
**How:** *from such turn away... For of this sort are they which creep into houses, and lead captive silly women laden with sins, led away with divers lusts; Ever learning, and never able to come to the knowledge of the truth. Now as Jannes and Jambres withstood Moses, so do these also* <u>*resist the truth*</u>*: men of corrupt minds reprobate concerning the truth,"* (2 Timothy 3:1-8).

**Gedaliah's error:** Gedaliah was a lover of his own self.
**The right path:** *O foolish Galatians, who hath bewitched you, that ye should not obey the truth; they shall turn away their ears from the truth, and shall be turned unto fables; because they receive not the love of the truth that they might be saved.*
**The defeat of the flesh:** Queen Esther was in a similar situation as Gedaliah. Her uncle, Mordecai, informed her of a plot by Haman to destroy their people (the Jews). He asked her to go and intercede with the king on behalf of their nation. Initially, Queen Esther withstood his words. Speaking from her flesh, she informed Mordecai that there was a law that forbade her from going to the king, without being summoned. Mordecai explained to her that a nation would be destroyed if she didn't take the risk. Being provoked unto love, Esther fasted and prayed; received the favor of the king, and saved herself and her nation. She turned away from self-love.
**Commentary:** Self-love is evident when truth is resisted.

## Gedaliah was in Unbelief

**What:** *"Take heed, brethren,*
**Why:** *Lest there be in any of you an evil heart of unbelief... in departing from the living God.*
**How:** *But exhort one another daily, while it is called to day; lest any of you be hardened through the deceitfulness of sin. For we are made partakers of Christ, if we hold the beginning of our confidence stedfast unto the end,"*
(Hebrews 3:12-14).

**Gedaliah's error**: Gedaliah had no rest for his soul... he was in unbelief.
**The right path:** (see Hebrews 3 & 4). *"To whom sware he that they should not enter into his rest, but to them that believed not, so we see that they could not enter in because of unbelief. Let us therefore fear, lest, a promise being left us of entering into his rest, any of you should seem to come short of it. For unto us was the gospel preached, as well as unto them: but the word preached did not profit them, not being mixed with faith in them that heard it. For we which have believed do enter into rest; although the works were finished from the foundation of the world."*
**The defeat of the flesh:** In 2 Kings 5:1-14, Naaman, the captain of the Syrian army, was sent by the king of Syria to be recovered of his leprosy. When he reached the man of God, he was told to go wash in Jordan seven times: *"But Naaman was wroth, and went away, and said, Behold, I thought, He will surely come out to me, and stand, and call on the name of the Lord his God, and strike his hand over the place, and recover the leper...So he turned and went away in a rage. And his servants came near, and spake unto him, and said, My father... Then went he down, and dipped himself seven times in Jordan, according to the saying of the man of God: and his flesh came again like unto the flesh of a little child, and he was clean."* Naaman almost missed God. Although his thoughts differed with the method used by the man of God, he submitted himself, and turned from his unbelief.
**Commentary:** Heeding an exhortation prevents unbelief.

# Unbelief

## A Subtle Enemy and the Single Most Cause of Defeat

Unbelief causes our hearts to faint: When Joseph's brothers told their father (Jacob) that Joseph was alive and that he was governor over all the land of Egypt, the Bible says: *"Jacob's heart fainted, for he believed them not,"* (Genesis 45:26).

Unbelief causes us to miss the promise land: *"And the Lord Spake unto Moses and Aaron, Because ye believed me not, to sanctify me in the eyes of the children of Israel, therefore ye shall not bring this congregation into the land which I have given them,"* (Numbers 20:12).

Unbelief causes God to change His plans for our life: *"Likewise when the Lord sent you from Kadeshbarnea, saying, Go up and possess the land which I have given you; then ye rebelled against the commandment of the Lord your God, and ye believed him not, nor hearkened to his voice,"* (Deut. 9:23). *"Ye shall know my breach of promise,"* (Numbers 14:34).

Unbelief causes us to belittle the land. God said: *"Yea, they despised the pleasant land, they believed not his word: But murmured in their tents, and hearkened not unto the voice of the Lord. Therefore he lifted up his hand against them, to overthrow them in the wilderness: To overthrow their seed also among the nations, and to scatter them in the lands,"* (Psalms 106:24-27).

Unbelief brings rebuke from our risen Savior: *"And they, when they had heard that he was alive, and had been seen of her, believed not. After that he appeared in another form unto two of them, as they walked, and went into the country. And they went and told it unto the residue: neither believed they them. Afterward he appeared unto the eleven as they sat at meat, and upbraided them with their unbelief and hardness of heart, because they believed not them which had seen him after he was risen,"* (Mark 16:11-14).

Luke 24:11 explained that: *"Their words seem to them as idle tales, and they believed them not."*

Unbelief causes us to require proof (sense evidence): *"The other disciples therefore said unto him, We have seen the Lord. But he said unto them, Except I shall see in his hands the print of the nails, and put my finger into the print of the nails, and thrust my hand into his side, <u>I will not believe</u>. And after eight days again his disciples were within, and Thomas with them: then came Jesus, the doors being shut, and stood in the midst, and said, Peace be unto you. Then saith he to Thomas, Reach hither thy finger, and behold my hands; and reach hither thy hand, and thrust it into my side: and be not faithless, but believing. And Thomas answered and said unto him, My Lord and my God. Jesus saith unto him, Thomas, because thou hast seen me, thou hast believed: <u>blessed are they that have not seen, and yet have believed</u>,"* (John 20:25-29).

By contrast, the book of Hebrews speaks of the harlot, Rahab, who refused to join the group of unbelievers: *"By faith the harlot Rahab perished not with them that believed not, when she had received the spies with peace,"* (Hebrews 11:31).

## Gedaliah was a Victim of Pleasant Knowledge

**What:** *"When wisdom entereth into thine heart*
**Why:** *and knowledge is pleasant unto thy soul;*
**How:** *Discretion shall preserve thee, understanding shall keep thee: To deliver thee from the way of the evil man, from the man that speaketh froward things,"* (Proverbs 2:10-12).

**Gedaliah's error:** Gedaliah failed to use discretion—he failed to search out the matter, as outlined in the book of Deuteronomy: *"Then shalt thou enquire, and make search, and ask diligently; and, behold, if it be truth, and the thing certain, that such abomination is wrought among you; Thou shalt surely smite the inhabitants of that city with the edge of the sword, destroying it utterly, and all that is therein, and the cattle thereof, with the edge of the sword,"* (Deuteronomy 13:14-15).

**The right path:** *"By faith Moses, when he was come to years, refused to be called the son of Pharaoh's daughter; Choosing rather to suffer affliction with the people of God, than to enjoy the pleasures of sin for a season; Esteeming the reproach of Christ greater riches than the treasures in Egypt: for he had respect unto the recompense of the reward,"* (Hebrews 11:24-26).

**The defeat of the flesh:** Joseph successfully dealt with the pleasant knowledge test when he refused the advances of Potiphar's wife: *"And it came to pass after these things, that his master's wife cast her eyes upon Joseph; and she said, lie with me. But he refused, and said unto his master's wife, Behold, my master wotteth not what is with me in the house, and he hath committed all that he hath to my hand; There is none greater in this house than I; neither hath he kept back anything from me but thee, because thou art his wife: how then can I do this great wickedness, and sin against God? And it came to pass, as she spake to Joseph day by day, that he hearkened not unto her, to lie by her, or to be with her,"* (Genesis 39:7-10).

**Commentary:** When knowledge is pleasant, caution is required.

## Gedaliah was a Debtor to the Flesh

**What:** *"We are debtors, not to the flesh, to live after the flesh.*
**Why:** *For if we live after the flesh, we shall die:*
**How:** *but if we through the spirit do mortify the deeds of the body, we shall live. For as many as are led by the Spirit of God, they are the sons of God,"* (Romans 8:12-14).

**Gedaliah's error**: Gedaliah refused to stand fast in the liberty.
**The right path:** *Stand fast in the liberty wherewith Christ has made you free; be not entangled again with the yoke of bondage; and fall from grace, but through the Spirit wait for the hope of righteousness by faith; Know you not, to whom you yield yourselves servants to obey, his servants you are to whom you obey; whether of sin unto death, or of obedience unto unrighteousness.*
**The defeat of the flesh:** In the kingdom of God, we guard our hearts by going from one level of faith to another level of faith. Mary, the mother of Jesus, exemplified this principle when she went to Jesus at the wedding of Cana and told Him: *"They have no more wine."* Mary was in faith when she shared this information. Jesus, testing her faith, said: *"Woman what have that to do with me, My time has not yet come."* Mary, staying in faith, turned to the servants and said: *"Whatever He says to you, do it,"* (John 2).

Mary could have said, "Oh, I must have missed God." If she had, she would have gone from faith to doubt. But our righteousness is revealed only from faith to faith. We become debtors to the flesh when we take our faith from: faith to doubt, faith to fear, or even faith to unbelief. Mary waited for the hope of righteousness by faith, but Gedaliah felt an allegiance to his flesh. Tied to his emotions, he had to serve his flesh.
**Commentary:** We perish when we do not mortify the root deception.

## Gedaliah's Errors of Omission

Gedaliah's <u>errors of omission</u> consist of things he failed to do: *"Therefore to him that knoweth to do good, and doeth it not, to him it is sin,"* (James 4:17). These errors arise from the hidden sins of the heart; they are the weightier matters.

### Gedaliah Failed to Guard His Heart from Pride

**What:** *"Keep (guard) our hearts with all diligence*
**Why:** *for out of it are the issues of life.*
**How:** *Put away from thee a froward mouth, and perverse lips put far from thee. Let thine eyes look right on, and let thine eyelid look straight before thee. Ponder the path of thy feet, and let all thy ways be established. Turn not to the right hand nor to the left remove thy foot from evil,"* (Proverbs 4:23-27).

In examining Gedaliah's errors of omission we find areas of negligence; things he failed to do. First and foremost, he failed to keep (guard) his heart. As a result, he became a victim of pride, where deception reigns. In Obadiah 1:3, God says: *"The pride of thine heart hath deceived thee..."* The Bible also points out that: *"A deceived heart has turned him aside, that he cannot deliver his soul..."* (Isaiah 44:20).

His pride would not allow him to receive information contrary to his own wisdom; his own feelings. By exalting his flesh, he fell prey to spiritual abasement. *"And whosoever shall exalt himself shall be abased; and he that humbles himself shall be exalted,"* (Matthew 23:12). Pride made him unstable; prone to err, and lawless.

Mankind is subject to the physical laws of the universe whether or not we are aware of a particular violation of them. Spiritual laws work the same way. Violation of spiritual laws causes our foundation to be out of course, and we will walk in darkness (see Psalms 82:5). Gedaliah, having spoken what he knew naturally (the flesh can only speak the natural), corrupted himself (see Jude 1:10). He was not aware of the consequences of being deceived by his own heart, and consequences occur, because laws are broken.

The Bible tells us that the heart is designed to speak what is inside of it, in abundance. If the heart is filled with unbelief, then words of unbelief will flow from the mouth: *"For, out of the abundance of the heart, the mouth speaks,"* (Matthew 12:34). And, when the mouth has spoken, either angels come to fulfil our faith-filled spoken words, or fallen angels come for words of unbelief. We are justified or condemned by the very words that we allow to come from our mouths—they show the condition of the heart. Gedaliah's heart gave fallen angels dominion over his life. He reaped the harvest (judgment) of the words he spoke.

The Bible tells the story of a young man who was similar to Gedaliah. He too, being lifted up in pride, was therefore unable to hear wisdom. Consequently, he had the same result. His name was Asahel, and his story is told in 2 Samuel 2:14-30.

Joab and Abner were captains of the armies of opposing kingdoms. During a type of mock battle, Abner's young men fought against Joab's young men; skill levels being equal. The Bible says that Asahel, the younger brother of Joab, was *light of foot*. He decided to pursue after Abner, the captain of the opposing kingdom. Abner tried to deter him saying: *"Turn aside to the right hand or to the left, and lay thee hold on one of the young men, and take thee his armour. But Asahel would not turn aside from following him. And Abner said again to Asahel, Turn thee aside from following me: where for should I smite thee to the ground? How then should I hold up my face to Joab thy brother? Howbeit he refused to turn aside: wherefore Abner with the hinder end of the spear smote him under the fifth rib, that the spear came out behind him; and he fell down there and died in the same place."*

Like Gedaliah, Asahel, being blinded by pride, failed to guard his own heart. Whether our pride is due to our own wisdom, our position, our talents, our accomplishments, or our traditions, the results are the same. Pride refuses to allow us to live the good life.

## Gedaliah Failed to let no Man Deceive Him with Vain Words

**What:** *"Let no man deceive you with vain words.*

**Why:** *For because of these things comes the wrath of God upon the children of disobedience.*

**How:** *Be not ye partakers…walk as children of light…proving what is acceptable to the Lord,"* (Ephesians 5:6-10).

Gedaliah allowed himself to be deceived with vain words (empty words that came from his flesh). The Bible says: *"The natural man receives not the things of the spirit of God for they are foolishness to him; neither can he know them, because they are spiritually discerned,"*
(1 Corinthians 2:14).

In the book of Numbers, chapters 13 &14, God promised to give the children of Israel the promise land. Moses sent one leader from each of the twelve tribes to go and spy out the land. When the leaders returned, ten of them brought back an evil report. They told the children of Israel that the land was indeed a good land, filled with milk and honey; they even brought back a sample of the fruit that was in the land. But, they said there were also giants in the land. They then named the giants and concluded that they themselves were as grasshoppers compared to them. When the congregation heard their evil report, they lifted up their voices and cried. They would later confess that their brothers had discouraged their hearts. Although two leaders tried to convince them that the land could still be taken, because God was on their side; the children of Israel would not allow themselves to be persuaded. They had already received the evil report; vain words had already lodged in their hearts.

Scripture says that we draw the wrath of God when we allow ourselves to be deceived by vain words: words that lead us astray and cause us to walk in the imagination of our own hearts. The children of Israel had to wander in the wilderness for 40 years. And we know that self-deception cost Gedaliah his life.

## Gedaliah Failed to Feed his Hungry Soul

**What:** *"They wandered in the wilderness in a solitary way; they found no city to dwell in.*
**Why:** *Hungry and thirsty, their soul fainted in them.*
**How:** *Then they cried unto the LORD in their trouble, and he delivered them out of their distresses,"* (Psalms 107:4-6).

In Matthew 25:31-46, Jesus tells the parable of the sheep and the goats. He said that at the end of time, He would separate the sheep from the goats. The sheep would be placed on His right hand and the goats on His left: *"Then shall the King say unto them on his right hand, Come, ye blessed of my Father, inherit the kingdom prepared for you from the foundation of the world: For I was an hungred, and ye gave me meat: I was thirsty, and ye gave me drink: I was a stranger, and ye took me in: Naked, and ye clothed me: I was sick, and ye visited me: I was in prison, and ye came unto me. Then shall the righteous answer him, saying, Lord, when saw we thee an hungred, and fed thee? or thirsty, and gave thee drink? When saw we thee a stranger, and took thee in? or naked, and clothed thee? Or when saw we thee sick, or in prison, and came unto thee? And the King shall answer and say unto them, Verily I say unto you, Inasmuch as ye have done it unto one of the least of these my brethren, ye have done it unto me."*

*"Then shall he say also unto them on the left hand, Depart from me, ye cursed, into everlasting fire, prepared for the devil and his angels: For I was an hungred, and ye gave me no meat: I was thirsty, and ye gave me no drink: I was a stranger, and ye took me not in: naked, and ye clothed me not: sick, and in prison, and ye visited me not. Then shall they also answer him, saying, Lord, when saw we thee an hungred, or athirst, or a stranger, or naked, or sick, or in prison, and did not minister unto thee? Then shall he answer them, saying, Verily I say unto you, Inasmuch as ye did it not to one of the least of these, ye did it not to me. And these shall go away into everlasting punishment: but the righteous into life eternal,"* (Matthew 25:41-46).

Both groups had hungry souls, but the sheep ministered to their souls, by receiving the truth; the goats did not. 1 Peter 2:25 says: *"The sheep returned to the Shepherd and Bishop of their souls, when they went astray."* They saw the need to return to the One who could help feed their hungry souls, so that they could help others.

In Psalms 42:5, David spoke to his hungry soul, saying: *"Why are thou cast down, O my soul? And why are thou disquieted in me? Hope thou in God for I shall yet praise him for the help of His countenance."*

The hungry soul is in need of the countenance of God. Numbers 6:25-26, says there is peace in the countenance of God as He makes His face to shine on us; giving us gladness, joy, and favor.

Gedaliah had a hungry soul also, but he refused to receive the truth that would have preserved him. When we, as individuals, are full, we will even push away from dessert. But when the soul is hungry, we are not particular about what we eat. To the hungry soul, even a lie is sweet. Proverbs 27:7 says it best: *"The full soul loatheth the honeycomb; but to the hungry soul every bitter thing is sweet."* Because he did not minister to his soul, he could not save the remnant of those not taken into captivity. Being hungry and thirsty, his soul fainted in him (see Psalms 107:5).

The Bible tells of a time when Ziklag, the place where David and his mighty men were living, was invaded by the Amalekites and burned with fire. The Amalekites had also taken their families captive. David was greatly distressed: *"For the people spoke of stoning him because the soul of all the people was grieved, every man for his sons and for his daughters,"* (1 Samuel 30:6).

But David encouraged himself in the Lord. He asked God two questions: *"Shall I pursue after this troop? shall I overtake them? And He answered him, Pursue: for thou shall surely overtake them, and without fail recover all. So David went, he and the six hundred men that were with him....and David recovered all that the Amalekites had carried away: and David recused his two wives. And there was nothing lacking to them, neither*

17

*small nor great, neither sons nor daughters, neither spoil nor anything that they had taken to them: David recovered all,"* (1 Samuel 30:1-19). David said God's <u>countenance</u> gave him help. After David fed his soul, he was able to deliver others.

From time to time our souls may need to be encouraged, just based on the situations of life. The soul, being exposed to this natural world, will be tested by the circumstances of life. Knowing how to be abased and how to abound is a part of the maturation process. When we take the responsibility to feed our hungry souls, God will always cause us to triumph in Christ.

God gave me a dream recently where I saw myself going north. Inside of me was a set of balancing scales. I noticed that the right side of the scale always stayed upright (being my spirit), but the left side tended to droop down from time to time (being my soul). I noticed that every time that I said encouraging words of God, the left side would pick back up. As I continued walking, it would drop; but words of faith made it return to a balanced state. Later that week, I found myself speaking to my soul every time it needed encouragement. Psalms 107:9 says: *"He satisfies the longing soul, and fills the hungry soul with goodness."*

The sheep, when they were hungry, fed on the goodness of God and encouraged themselves. When they were thirsty, they refreshed themselves in the praises of God. When they felt estranged from the covenant, they fed on His promises. Naked, they clothed themselves with the robe of righteousness. Sick, they sought God's presence, and worshipped Him. In prison, they came to their own senses. And, after they were converted, they strengthened others.

## Gedaliah Failed to Heed the Call to Virtue

**What:** *"Whatsoever things are true, whatsoever things are honest, whatsoever things are just, whatsoever things are pure, whatsoever things are lovely, and whatsoever things are of a good report.*
**Why:** *if there be any virtue, if there be any praise*
**How:** *think on these things,"* (Philippians 4:8).


A woman who was diseased with an issue of blood for twelve years came behind Jesus and touched the hem of His garment. For she said: *"Within herself, if I may but touch His garment, I shall be whole,"* (Matthew 9:20-22). In Luke's version, he added that: *"When she came in behind Jesus and touched the border of His garment, immediately her issue of blood stanched. And Jesus said, who touched me? ...Somebody has touched me for I perceive that virtue is gone out of me, and when He saw her, he said, Daughter, be of good comfort; thy faith has made you whole,"* (Luke 8:46).

Speaking faith-filled words allows virtue to flow, and virtue allows us to partake of the divine nature of God. The Bible said that for twelve years she had spent all her living on physicians—neither could be healed of any. In other words, her condition was terminal. The only solution to her condition was virtue. And virtue can only flow from thoughts that do not defile the heart. 2 Peter 1:3-4 says: *"Of him that hath called us to glory and virtue... that by these ye might be partakers of the divine nature, having escaped the corruption that is in the world through lust."* We partake of God's nature as we allow virtuous thought to flow from the heart.

Philippians 4:8 says that virtue flows as we think on things that are: true, honest, just, pure, lovely, and of a good report. If your thought is not of a good report, you can't think on it: *"For as he thinketh in his heart, so is he,"* (Proverbs 23:7).

The first criterion for virtue to flow in a life-or-death situation is truth. Because Gedaliah resisted the truth, the virtue that was necessary for his deliverance was not available for him. The Bible said: *"He believed him not."* The woman with the issue of blood made sure that her thoughts were virtuous; they released the power of creation to operate on her behalf. Her faith-filled thoughts alone qualified her and made her whole.

Our thoughts place us in our spirit or in our flesh; however, dominion flows only from the spirit. The kingdom within us is faith-based and releases its power through thoughts that line up with the word of God. Gedaliah forfeited his dominion when he failed to believe. He walked in agreement with his flesh, and thoughts from the flesh have no power to deliver.

We sometimes pride ourselves on predicting the behavior of others. We say things like: "I'll apply for that job, but they won't hire me," or, "I'll ask for some money, but she'll just say no." When we get just what we thought, we say, "I knew it," not realizing that we have sabotaged the kingdom within us. If the woman with the issue of blood had said, "I will touch his garment, but I still won't get healed," she too, would have gotten just what she thought, and we would not be writing about her.

The other day I picked up some hydrocortisone cream from the doctor for my youngest son. I took one look at the medicine and thought; *we are going to need a second tube.* Sure enough, later on we needed another tube. I got the second tube and thought; *if I need another one, I'll just ask.* Two weeks later, I needed another application. The doctor was taken aback because he was certain that two tubes would have been more than enough. He questioned the nurse, who then questioned me, saying, "The doctor was sure you had enough." By then I realized what had happened. I thought that it would take more time for the medicine to work, and it did. By doing so, I inadvertently slowed down the healing process.

The Bible tells us that Ruth, on the other hand, worked with her thought of dominion to obtain favor with Boaz. Prior to going into the field, Ruth said unto Naomi, her mother in law: *"Let me now to go the field and glean ears of corn after him in whose sight I shall find grace* (favor),*"* (Ruth 2:2).

She then went and obtained so much favor that the owner of the field married her. Boaz was able to marry Ruth because she spoke words that were in line with the will of God. Ruth's words allowed virtue to flow. Gedaliah's words did not.

## Gedaliah Failed to do Justice and Judgment

**What:** *"In transgressing and lying against the Lord, and departing away from our God, speaking oppression and revolt, conceiving an uttering from the heart words of falsehood. And judgment is turned away backward and justice standeth afar off:*
**Why:** *for truth is fallen in the street, and equity cannot enter. Yea, truth faileth; and he that departeth from evil maketh himself a prey: and the Lord saw it,*
**How:** *and it displeased him that there was no judgment. And he saw that there was no man, and wondered that there was no intercessor: therefore his arm brought salvation unto him; and his righteousness, it sustained him,"*
(Isaiah 59:13-16).


Gedaliah was not valiant for truth. When deception is tolerated, God takes it personally, because He cannot fulfill His promises; His word is on the line. When the children of Israel were deceived into thinking that they could not possess the promise land, God told them that they would know his *breach of promise.* Their unbelief caused God to change his plans for their lives.

Executing judgment is a vital part of maintaining justice. Gedaliah died prematurely because he did not execute judgment on his own thoughts. The children of Israel failed to take the promise land because they did not execute judgment on their thoughts, fears, and unbelief. We know that they were in unbelief because their children, under Joshua's leadership, did possess the same land that they themselves had despised.

Being deceived, Gedaliah could not intercede for the people to execute judgment on their behalf. In Ezekiel 22:30, God said: *"And I sought for a man among them, that should make up the hedge, and stand in the gap before me for the land, that I should not destroy it: but I found none."* God looked for an intercessor to effectively render judgment to the enemy.

In Genesis 18:19, God in discussing Abraham's faithfulness, stated: *"I know him, he will command his children and his household after him, and they shall keep the way of the Lord to do justice and judgment; that the Lord may bring upon Abraham that which he has spoken of him."* God proved Abraham's faithfulness when He was about to destroy Sodom and Gomorrah. He shared His heart about the cry of that nation with Abraham, who responded by interceding. Although God was not able to find even ten righteous in that land, Lot and his family (relatives of Abraham) were delivered.

In Deuteronomy 13:14-15, God taught the Israelites to take heed to what they heard: *"Then shalt thou enquire, and make search, and ask diligently; and, behold, if it be truth, and the thing certain, that such abomination is wrought among you; then thou shall surely, smite the inhabitants of that city with the edge of the sword, destroying it utterly, and all that is therein, and the cattle thereof, with the edge of the sword..."* Gedaliah refused to make inquiry to ascertain the truth. His failure to follow the 'take heed to what you hear' precept cost him dearly.

In Jeremiah 21:12, God commands us to execute judgment in the morning: *"O house of David, thus saith the Lord; Execute judgment in the morning, and deliver him that is spoiled out of the hand of the oppressor, lest my fury go out like fire, and burn that none can quench it, because of the evil of your doings."*

When deceived by the fig tree, Jesus executed judgment saying: *"And Jesus answered and said unto it, No man eat fruit of thee hereafter forever. And his disciples heard it... And in the morning, as they passed by, they saw the fig tree dried up from the roots. And Peter calling to remembrance saith unto him, Master, behold, the fig tree which thou cursed is withered away,"* (Mark 11:14-21).

Jesus demonstrated that all deception must be judged. It's not enough to say; "Oh, I was wrong," the erroneous thought of the heart must be punished.

## Gedaliah Failed to Take Captive Every Thought

**What:** *"For though we walk in the flesh, we do not war after the flesh:*
**Why:** *(for the weapons of our warfare are not carnal, but mighty through God to the pulling down of strong holds;)*
**How:** *casting down imaginations, and every high thing that exalteth itself against the knowledge of God, and brining into captivity every thought to the obedience of Christ,"* (2 Corinthians 10:3-5).

Thoughts of unbelief, doubt, and fear, must be kept under the radar of faith. This means we must guard our eye gate, our ear gate and our mouth gate from contaminating influences. This responsibility requires us to: *"Take heed what you hear: with what measure you mete, it shall be measured to you: and unto you that hear shall more be given. For he that hath, to him shall be given: and he that has not, from him shall be taken even that which he has,"* (Mark 4:24-25). This scripture implies that failure to examine what you hear will cause you loss, but to those who hear (receive), they will get more: more to validate their knowledge, or more to invalidate it.

As governors of our thought life, we must bring every thought to the obedience of Christ. Though Gedaliah was governor of the land, he failed to govern his own thoughts. Even when approached by Ishmael, he failed to open his mouth. Proverbs 24:7 says: *"Wisdom is too high for a fool, because he opens not his mouth at the gate."*

The flesh, like Satan, transforms itself into an angel of light (see 2 Corinthians 11:14). Therefore, we must take every thought captive to test if this message is in line with the written word of God. We can also use the multitude of counselors to test the message. The Bible instructs us to: *"Prove all things and hold fast to that which is good,"* (1 Thessalonians 5:21). We must take responsibility to not be deceived by our thoughts.

In Luke 4:1-13, Jesus, during His time of temptation, took captive each thought by the tempter with the words: *"It is written."* When the tempter, knowing that Jesus was hungry, after his forty day fast, tempted him with a desire of the flesh: *"Command this stone that it be made bread."* Jesus answered: *"It is written, That man shall not live by bread alone, but by every word of God."*

With the second thought, the tempter took Jesus up to a high pinnacle and said: *"All this power will I give thee, and the glory of them: for that is delivered unto me; and to whomsoever I will I give it. If thou therefore wilt worship me, all shall be thine."* Jesus answered and said: *"Thou shalt worship the Lord thy God, and him only shalt thou serve."* Jesus demonstrated the power of right speaking.

Finally, the thought came to Jesus by way of the tempter saying: *"If thou be the Son of God, cast thyself down from hence: For it is written, He shall give his angels charge over thee, to keep thee: And in their hands they shall bear thee up, lest at any time thou dash thy foot against a stone. And Jesus answering said unto him, It is said, Thou shalt not tempt the Lord thy God."*

Yes, the enemy will use scriptures (wrongly applied) to get us out of the will of God. Thoughts from the tempter were filled with the lust of the flesh, the lust of the eyes, and the pride of life (see 1 John 2:16), but they were not filled with faith. Jesus knew he could not separate himself from His faith.

When I pondered the faith process, the Holy Spirit reminded me of the childhood game called, Simon Says. It is a game where you can only do exactly what Simon says: "Simon says, Jump," so you jump. "Simon says, Hop," so you hop. "Simon says, Look up," so you look up. "Look down." No, you continue to look up because Simon didn't say it (It was an angel of light).

There was no faith in the last command. When there is no faith, that means you are not fully persuaded. Faith is necessary to please God. In 1 Kings 19:11-12, Elijah found faith only in a still small voice.

## Gedaliah Failed to Turn Himself

**What:** *"Wherefore let him that thinketh he standeth take heed lest he fall.*
**Why:** *There hath no temptation taken you but such as is common to man: but God is faithful, who will not suffer you to be tempted above that ye are able; but will with the temptation also make a way to escape, that ye may be able to bear it.*
**How:** *Wherefore, my dearly beloved, flee from idolatry,"* (1 Cor. 10:12-14).

The Bible says all temptations are common to man, but He will always give us a way of escape that we may be able to bear the temptation. In essence, when we are tempted to go the wrong way, we will be given a prompting to perfect the lack in our faith. If we are tempted to fear, God will show us the way of peace. If we are tempted with unbelief, He will give us wisdom to strengthen our faith.

Years ago, I worked with a froward (contrary) type of individual. Initially, I responded with an eye for an eye attitude; however, as I sought biblical help during my time of devotion, the Holy Spirit gave me the perfect scripture. He had me *turn the other cheek* and respond with kingdom wisdom. It worked extremely well. I learned that each of us is afflicted with the same issues of life, but there is victory for those who <u>turn</u> to God and follow his way of escape.

The Bible identifies several individuals who <u>turned</u> themselves from the flesh to following the prompting of the Holy Spirit. Consider Boaz, in the book of Ruth. He was initially frightened when he found Ruth lying at his feet, but the Bible says he turned himself: *"And when Boaz had eaten and drunk, and his heart was merry, he went to lie down at the end of the heap of corn: and she came softly, and uncovered his feet, and laid her down. And it came to pass at midnight, that the man was <u>afraid,</u> and <u>turned himself</u>: and, behold, a woman lay at his feet. And he said, Who art thou? And she answered, I am Ruth thine handmaid: spread therefore thy skirt over thine handmaid; for thou art a near kinsman,"* (Ruth 3:7-9).

Boaz turned himself from fear to faith. He turned from responding in his flesh to responding in his spirit. Receiving the thought from his spirit, he was able to strategically handle the nearer-kinsman and secure Ruth for his wife.

To turn is to go from walking in your flesh to walking in your dominion; however, you can also go in the other direction. In Psalms 78:41, God says: *"Yea, they turned back and tempted God, and limited the Holy One of Israel."* Whenever we turn and walk in the flesh, we limit the power of God, and when we walk after the flesh, Jeremiah says we become a strange vine: *"I had planted thee a noble vine, wholly a right seed: how then art thou turned into the degenerate plant of a strange vine unto me,"* (Jeremiah 2:21).

In Genesis, Joseph made himself strange to his brothers. He went from being in the spirit to the flesh: *"And Joseph was the governor over the land, and he it was that sold to all the people of the land: and Joseph's brethren came, and bowed down themselves before him with their faces to the earth. And Joseph saw his brethren, and he knew them, but made himself strange unto them, and spake roughly unto them; and he said unto them, Whence come ye? And they said, From the land of Canaan to buy food. And Joseph knew his brethren, but they knew not him,"* (Genesis 42:6-8). Later, Joseph made himself known unto his brothers.

King Solomon, although wise, had fallen into the flesh. His wives had turned his heart from following God; however, his wisdom remained in him. While reflecting on the vanity of life, he needed to access that wisdom. Solomon said: *"And I turned myself to behold wisdom, and madness, and folly: for what can the man do that cometh after the king? even that which hath been already done. Then I saw that wisdom excelleth folly, as far as light excelleth darkness,"* (see Ecclesiastes 2:9-13).

King Saul found that when he turned himself, he was able to vex the enemy at will: *"So Saul took the kingdom over Israel, and fought against all his enemies on every side, against Moab, and against the children of Ammon, and against Edom, and against the kings of Zobah, and against the*

*Philistines: and whithersoever he turned himself, he vexed them,"* (1 Samuel 14:47).

When Mary Magdalene discovered that Jesus' grave was empty, she assumed that the body had been stolen. Being in unbelief, she was unable to see Jesus even after he appeared to her. She eventually <u>turned</u> herself and was able to see Him: *"They say unto her, Woman, why weepest thou? She saith unto them, Because they have taken away my Lord, and I know not where they have laid him. And when she had thus said, she turned herself back, and saw Jesus standing, and knew not that it was Jesus. Jesus saith unto her, Woman, why weepest thou? whom seekest thou? She, supposing him to be the gardener saith unto him, Sir, if thou have borne him hence, tell me where thou hast laid him, and I will take him away. Jesus saith unto her, Mary. <u>She turned herself,</u> and saith unto him, Rabboni; which is to say, Master. Jesus saith unto her, Touch me not; for I am not yet ascended to my Father: but go to my brethren, and say unto them, I ascend unto my Father, and your Father; and to my God, and your God. Mary Magdalene came and told the disciples that she had seen the Lord, and that he had spoken these things unto her,"* (John 20:13-18).

Gedaliah received a prompting also, but failed to yield to it. God is faithful to give each of us the promised way of escape. However, when we fail to humble ourselves and turn from our wicked ways, we give the flesh dominion. Numbers 14:43 says: *"For the Amalekites and the Canaanites are there before you, and ye shall fall by the sword: because ye are <u>turned</u> away from the Lord, therefore the Lord will not be with you."* Mary Magdalene <u>turned</u> from her unbelief and her tale testifies against Gedaliah.

Deuteronomy says we are to: *"Take heed to yourselves, that your heart be not deceived, and ye <u>turn aside,</u> and serve other gods, and worship them; And then the Lord's wrath be kindled against you, and he shut up the heaven, that there be no rain, and that the land yield not her fruit; and lest ye perish quickly from off the good land which the Lord giveth you,"* (Deuteronomy 11:16-17).

## Gedaliah did not Submit to Another
## in the Fear of the Lord

**What:** *"Be ye not unwise*
**Why:** *but understand what the will of the Lord is.*
**How:** *And be not drunk with wine, wherein is excess; but be filed with the Spirit; Speaking to yourselves in psalms and spiritual songs, singing and making melody in your heart to the Lord; Giving thanks always for all things unto God and the Father in the name of our Lord; <u>Submitting yourselves one to another in the fear of the Lord</u>,"* (Ephesians 5:17-21).

Because Gedaliah lacked humility, he was unable to submit one to another in the fear of the Lord; and without humility, you can't receive the truth (see 1Peter 5:5). The word has to be received as a seed. If we have no capacity to hold a seed, surely we can't receive more. Humility allows us to operate in a spirit of meekness. Meekness is a fruit of the spirit, against such there is no law—the flesh has no recourse against the fruit of meekness. Humility would have rendered judgment on Gedaliah's flesh.

In 2 Kings 5:1-14, Naaman, the captain of the Syrian army, was sent by the king of Syria to be recovered of his leprosy. When he reached the man of God, he was told to wash in Jordan seven times: *"But Naaman was wroth, and went away, and said, Behold, I thought, He will surely come out to me, and stand, and call on the name of the Lord his God, and strike his hand over the place, and recover the leper. Are not Abana and Pharpar, rivers of Damascus, better than all the waters of Israel? may I not wash in them, and be clean? So he turned and went away in a rage. And his <u>servants came near, and spake unto him</u>, and said, My father, if the prophet had bid thee do some great thing, wouldest thou not have done it? how much rather then, when he saith to thee, Wash, and be clean? Then <u>went he down,</u> and dipped himself seven times in Jordan, according to the saying of the man of*

*God: and his flesh came again like unto the flesh of a little child, and he was clean."*

Naaman's flesh told him that other waters were better. But when he obeyed, and submitted to his servants, he was clean. Humility calls for us to abase our pride and submit to wisdom that is against our own personal perceptions.

The story is told, in John chapter 11, about the time when Jesus raised Lazarus from the dead. Although Lazarus came forth from the grave, he was still bound in grave clothes and could not free himself. Jesus told the disciple to loose him. Lazarus had to trust others before he could be set free. This took humility.

Jesus told us that unless we become converted (loosed from our grave clothes; another type of flesh) and come as little children, we cannot enter into the kingdom of heaven. Little children are wise enough to humble themselves in order to receive the help they need to grow to maturity. Our grave clothes are not visible to us, for our minds have been blinded (see 2 Corinthians 4:4), but they are glaring to others and must be removed before growth and deliverance can take place.

Gedaliah was unaccustomed to the yoke of submitting one to another. This made him more inclined to trust himself. Being unequally yoked to his flesh, his emotions were under siege by unbelief. He had received no information outside of himself that would have contradicted Johanan's report. Gedaliah was trying to serve two masters: loving the one and hating the other; he was a servant of God, but serving his flesh.

## Gedaliah Failed to Examine Himself

**What:** *"Examine yourselves,*

**Why:** *whether ye be in the faith;*

**How:** *prove your own selves. Know ye not your own selves, how that Jesus Christ is in you, except ye be reprobates? But I trust that ye shall know that we are not reprobates,"* (2 Corinthians 13:5-6).

In 1 Kings 19, Elijah, in attempting to follow an instruction by God, encountered some interference, which could have potentially gotten him off course. Picking up the story in verse eleven, God said: *"…Go forth, and stand upon the mount before the LORD. And, behold, the LORD passed by, and a great and strong wind rent the mountains, and brake in pieces the rocks before the LORD; but the LORD was not in the wind: and after the wind an earthquake; but the LORD was not in the earthquake: And after the earthquake a fire; but the LORD was not in the fire: and after the fire a still small voice. And it was so, when Elijah heard it…,"* (1 Kings 19:11-13).

A number of forces attempted to get Elijah's attention, but as he examined himself, faith was only found in the still small voice. We are called to challenge our thoughts, beliefs, and ideas; to prove whether or not we are under the influence of grace or the law, the fruit of the Spirit or the flesh. 1 Thessalonians 5:21 says, *"Prove all things; hold fast that which is good."* We must examine whether our thoughts are in line with the word of God, and the will of God.

Ephesians 5:17 reminds us to: *"Be ye not unwise, but understanding what the will of the Lord is."*

1 Corinthians 14:10 says: *"There are, it may be, so many kinds of voices in the world, and none of them is without signification."* This is a call to sanctify every voice, and wait for the voice of faith—the still small voice.

This is where Gedaliah's failure cost him his life. Voices heralding pleasant knowledge, facts or otherwise, must be sanctified. The proper order for partaking of any fruit—buying into something is:

it has to be <u>pleasant to the sight</u>—in line with God's vision for us; and, <u>good for food</u>—not false doctrine (see Genesis 2:9). When Eve reversed this order, she fell short of the glory of God, and into sin. The Bible said: *"And when the woman saw that the tree was <u>good for food</u>, and that it was <u>pleasant to the eyes</u>, and a tree to be desired to make one wise, she took of the fruit thereof, and did eat, and gave also unto her husband with her; and he did eat,"* (Genesis 3:6).

So did Gedaliah. He bought into the information that was sold to him by his flesh, without examining it.

However, the Bible does identify others who have reaped the benefits of self-examination. King Saul attempted to give David his amour to use in fighting Goliath. David tried on the armour—he listened; and had to put it off because he had not proved it. *"And Saul armed David with his armour, and he put an helmet of brass upon his head; also he armed him with a coat of mail. And David girded his sword upon his armour, and he assayed to go; for he had not proved it. And David said unto Saul, I cannot go with these; for I have not proved them. And David put them off him,"* (1 Samuel 17:38-39). David examined himself and chose to use the armour—the wisdom, God provided. With that armour he defeated Goliath.

In 1 Kings 10:1-7, the queen of Sheba did not believe the report she had heard about King Solomon. So, she decided to prove him with hard questions. *"And when the queen of Sheba heard of the fame of Solomon concerning the name of the LORD, she came to prove him with hard questions."* Afterwards, she said: *"Howbeit I believed not the words, until I came, and mine eyes had seen it…"* Solomon opened the eyes of her understanding. The queen of Sheba admitted that she believed not, but being wise, did not want to risk being a reprobate; so she examined herself, by proving Solomon with hard questions. In essence, she put her beliefs on trial.

King Solomon said when he tried to walk independent of God, he failed to examine himself—wisdom was far from him. *"All this have I proved by wisdom: I said, I will be wise; but it was far from me,"* (Eccl. 7:23).

## Gedaliah's Condemnation

In 1 Samuel 17:4, the story is told of a champion out of the camp of the Philistines: Goliath, who was six cubits and a span. For forty days and forty nights he presented the Israelites with this challenge: *"Choose you a man for you, and let him come down to me. If he be able to fight with me, and to kill me, then will we be your servants: but if I prevail against him, and kill him, then shall ye be our servants, and serve us. And the Philistine said, I defy the armies of Israel this day; give me a man, that we may fight together,"* (1 Samuel 17:8-10).

Goliath is another type of flesh. The strategy that he espoused is a principle for takeover; we know it as *winner takes all*. Paul, in 1 Corinthians 9:24, explains it as a race: *"In a race runs all, but only one receives the prize."* Either the spirit man dominates, or your flesh reigns. Walking after the flesh places us under condemnation and makes us subject to the law of sin and death. Condemnation is the act of condemning; the judicial act of declaring one guilty and dooming the condemned to punishment—we are placed in bondage.

Gedaliah's own mouth condemned him, his own lips testified against him (see Job 15:6). Jesus, in John 3:18, said: *"He that believes on him is not condemned: but he that believed not is condemned already..."* Gedaliah's foundation of righteousness was already destroyed by the words that proceeded out of his mouth. He justified the wicked, his flesh; now evil shall not depart from his house. Gedaliah also condemned the just, the messenger. When we judge another, we condemn ourselves (see Romans 2:1).

Condemnation overthrows the structure of our spiritual authority. It cripples the believer with feelings of guilt, shame, fear, and remorse. When it is present, we cannot reign in our righteousness and faith cannot enter. Although we are the head, we operate as the tail, receiving counsel from the sin nature (the flesh). James 5:5-6 describes the strategies of this nature: *"You have lived in pleasure on earth, and been wanton; you have nourished your hearts, as in a day of slaughter. You have condemned and killed the just; and he does not resist you."* Gedaliah did not resist the thoughts coming from his own heart and not resisting made him a victim of himself. The story of Gedaliah tells of a man bound by his own thoughts, feelings, and insights and unable to see his own fragile state.

Gedaliah fell into condemnation both by unbelief and by condemning another. He was then subverted and became a victim of the flesh, awaiting punishment. According to the Bible, God spoke to Gedaliah's heart, informing him of the same information that was shared by the messenger, because Psalms 62:11 says: *"Once have God spoken, twice have I heard it."* The messenger's words were a confirmation to what had already been shared in Gedaliah's heart. Being in unbelief, he was not able to receive it. But, because God's word could not return void, He had to find those who would hear the word and keep it; those who could weather any storm. He had to find good ground.

*HE IS LIKE A MAN WHICH BUILT AN HOUSE,*

*AND DIGGED DEEP,*

*AND LAID THE FOUNDATION ON A ROCK:*

*AND WHEN THE FLOOD AROSE,*

*THE STREAM BEAT VEHEMENTLY UPON THAT HOUSE,*

*AND COULD NOT SHAKE IT:*

*FOR IT WAS FOUNDED UPON A ROCK.*


LUKE 6:48

# Chapter 2

## Ten Men

There is a parable in the Bible that talks about two builders. Throughout my Christian experience, this parable has given me the most enduring strength to handle the contradictions of life. The principle of this parable says that the circumstances of life are not the defeating factor, or the causation of failure. It addresses two builders, one wise and the other foolish, who were both faced with identical circumstances of life: the exact flood, the exact rain, and the exact wind. The wise man's house withstood the storm, but the foolish man's house fell. What has always been fascinating to me is that the storm didn't cause the house to fall (see Matthew 7:24-27).

An example of the parable of the two houses can be seen in the book of Ruth. The story is told of three women—each of them lost her husband. Naomi became bitter as a result of the loss, Orpah backslid and went back to serving other gods, but Ruth, being a hearer and doer of the word, was able to weather the storm. She kept her love and faith in God and received a full reward; including, marrying a wealthy land owner. Ruth eventually became the great grandmother of King David. In this story we can clearly see that the same circumstances hit each woman. They were each left poverty-stricken, but only one was unshakeable.

This parable is a tell-tale, because the same test that Gedaliah failed, there were ten men that passed. In Jeremiah chapter 41:8, the

Bible says: *"But ten men were found among them that said unto Ishmael: Slay us not: for we have treasure in the field, of wheat, and of barley, and of oil, and of honey. So he forbare, and slew them not among their brethren."* The Bible uses the conjunction <u>but</u> to show the contrast. There were many slain, including Gedaliah, but none of those who were slain resisted the evil. The primary difference between the two groups of men is that the ten men had what the Bible calls good ground: those who hear the word and keep it.

Matthew 13:3-23, explains the difficulty God has in finding those individuals who will listen to Him. Statically speaking, only one in four will hear Him and produce fruit. The other three have hearts that are distracted. Mathew illustrates why. When God speaks His word into our hearts, one allows the wicked one to steal it, another becomes offended; and the other allows the cares of this life, the deceitfulness of riches, or the lust of other things to choke His word and it becomes unfruitful. Because they fail to receive His word, these individuals become victims of their circumstances. Only those with good hearts heard and obeyed the command of the Father: resist Ishmael and inform him of the treasure.

God gave them all the same instruction (being no respecter of persons): plant wheat, barley, oil and honey, to disarm the threat. Those who heeded the command of God were ready for the impending storm. Having good hearts positioned the ten men to be hearers and doers of the word: *"(For not the hearers of the law are just before God, but the doers of the law shall be justified,"* (Romans 2:13). They were prepared for the storm.

As hearers and doers, the ten men communicated their faith, saying: *"We have treasure in the field."* Their treasure, the Bible says is: *"The fear of the Lord,"* (Isaiah 33:6). That is, they say what God tells them to say. After they communicated their faith, the Bible said, Ishmael slew them not among their brethren. Obeying God is the first line of defense.

## Passing the Field Test

Years ago, God gave my youngest son a dream about a young teen, who attended our church, being tested by the enemy. The young man failed because he had no answers for life's tests. In the next scene, his dream showed me working with the young man. He was later tested again and passed.

Understanding the dream, I knew that I was assigned to work with him, so I asked his parents for permission. They agreed, so I told him of the dream and informed him that I was going to prepare him to pass life's tests, which I did. It turns out that passing the foundational tests of life has to do with <u>receiving</u> instructional words of wisdom. Proverbs 23:23 exhorts us to: *"Buy the truth, and sell it not; also wisdom, and instruction, and understanding."* This scripture implies that the truth could be sold, but that would not be profitable.

In Matthew 13:44, Jesus said: *"Again, the kingdom of heaven as like unto treasure hid in a field; the which when a man hath found, he hideth, and for joy thereof goeth and selleth all that he hath, and buyeth that field."* The tests of life reveal themselves when you find yourself in the <u>field</u> (surrounded by worldly circumstances that cause you to speak words of fear, doubt, and unbelief). In Jeremiah 6:25, the Bible says: *"Go not forth into the field, nor walk by the way; for the sword of the enemy and fear is on every side."*

According to the Bible, the field portends the test to come.
- The serpent was in the field when Eve was tempted.
- Cain killed Abel in the field.
- Esau was faint in the field prior to selling his birthright.
- Joseph was wandering in the field looking for his brothers.
- The elder brother of the 'Prodigal Son' was angry in the field.

Solomon describes the field of the sluggard, those who refuse to take captive their thoughts (they are lying down on the job). He said: *"I went by the field of the sluggard, And by the vineyard of the man void of understanding; and, lo, it was all grown over with thorns, the face thereof was covered with nettles, and the stone wall thereof was broken down. Then I beheld, and considered well; I saw, and received instruction: Yet a little sleep, a little slumber, a little folding of the hands to sleep; so shall thy poverty come as a robber, and thy want as an armed man,"* (Proverbs 24:30-34). This scripture shows the need to cultivate the field of our hearts.

Conversely, the virtuous woman bought a field and with the fruit of her hand, she planted a vineyard (see Proverbs 31:16). She turned her field into a garden.

The field is the test; the treasure is what you get when you pass the test. To acquire the treasure you must sell all that is in the field; it is akin to having a yard sale. We must sell all doubt, all fear, all unbelief, and buy the truth.

### The Treasure in the Field

Queen Esther passed the "no greater love," test when she laid down her life for her people. Knowing the consequences (death) of appearing before the king without being summoned, she had to sell her fear. Queen Esther uncovered the treasure of love and inherited up to half of the kingdom.

The three Hebrew boys: Shadrach, Meshach, and Abednego passed the faithfulness test as they endured hardness as good solders. After being captured by the Babylonians, they refused to serve other gods or worship the golden image (things of the world) and faced a fiery furnace. They sold their cares and finding the treasure of faithfulness, they could not be destroyed.

Passing the patience test involves being willing to endure to the end: due season. Against hope (which was his field) Abraham believed in hope. He eventually <u>sold all</u> and uncovered the treasure of patience. Thus, he became heir of the world. Hebrews 6:15 says of Abraham: *"And so after he had patiently endured, he obtained the promise."*

According to the Bible, the field is the world. But, Abraham could not get his needs met through the world. There was no natural hope for him. Both he and his wife were beyond child-bearing age, and the desire of their hearts, to have a child, was outside the world's realm. But when he accessed the supernatural treasure of patience, he obtained the promise. Without the treasure, he could have not received the supernatural hope that was available for him. He would have lived his life beneath his privileges and childless.

The answers that the young man, in my son's dream, needed were not of this world, either; however, the tests of the field come to us all—ready or not. Without passing the test, (selling his field) he could not obtain the peace of mind that he desperately needed and deserved. He had to sell his field, which was inherited from birth and included situations and circumstances unique to him, in order to obtain the promise. Once he received instructional words of wisdom, he was prepared to pass life's tests of: doubt, unbelief and fear.

Notwithstanding, the promises of God are not automatic; it takes time to clear our fields. And, it takes time for fruit to be produced. A balance is required. If the process occurs outside of due season, desolation could occur. In talking to the children of Israel, God explained the reason for the delay of going into the promise land: *"I will not drive them out from before thee in one year, lest the land become <u>desolate</u> and the <u>beasts of the field</u> multiply against thee. By little and little I will drive them out from before thee, until thou be <u>increased,</u> and inherit the land,"* (Exodus 23:29-30).

The tests of life show the condition of the heart, and your ability to be abased. Passing the field test enables you to live the crucified life.

*AND THEY THAT ARE IN CHRIST'S*

*HAVE CRUCIFIED THE FLESH*

*WITH THE AFFECTIONS AND LUSTS.*

*IF WE LIVE IN THE SPIRIT,*

*LET US ALSO WALK IN THE SPIRIT*

*LET US NOT BE DESIROUS OF VAIN GLORY,*

*PROVOKING ONE ANOTHER,*

*ENVYING ONE ANOTHER.*

GALATIANS 5:24-26

# Chapter 3

## The Crucified Life

The Bible says we are defiled by our inner thought life and cast down by our own counsel. Luke 11:7 tells the parable of the man who knocks on the door of his friend, at midnight, asking for bread to feed another friend. The Bible says: *"And he from <u>within</u> shall answer and say, Trouble me not: the door is now shut, and my children are with me in bed; I cannot rise and give thee."* The man asked his friend, but the friend's flesh answered; giving an unlovely response. God describes the flesh as a land that is not clean—full of conspiracy. In Isaiah 10:14, the flesh brags that he has found our riches and that he is unopposed: none opened the mouth, or peeped him.

### The Flesh at Work

Years ago while my sister and I were in strife, she left to go out of town. After she was gone, I couldn't find my lipstick. I looked all around and could not find it. The flesh said, "Your sister took your lipstick and went out of town." This thought sounded logical; she could have taken it out of spite. I told my mom about the incident that caused the strife, including accusing my sister of taking my lipstick. Later that same day I found my lipstick. This experience has always stayed with me for one main reason: I realized that your thoughts lie to you; they wanted me to keep the strife going. Afterwards, I still found myself wrestling with thoughts, but I had at least peeped the flesh.

In Genesis, the flesh <u>lied</u> to Jacob. When Joseph's brothers brought the bloody coat of many colors to Jacob for him to identify, he said: *"It is my son's coat; an evil beast hath devoured him; Joseph is without doubt rent in pieces,"* (Genesis 37:33). Yet, Joseph was still alive, and he later became governor of the land of Egypt.

With Queen Esther, the flesh came as the <u>law</u> and told her that it was against the law to go into the king unannounced: *"All the king's servants, and the people of the king's provinces, do know, that whosoever, whether man or woman, shall come unto the king into the inner court, who is not called, there is one law of his to put him to death, except such to whom the king shall hold out the golden sceptre, that he may live: but I have not been called to come in unto the king these thirty days,"* (Esther 4:11). In fighting the flesh, Esther said: *"If I perish, I perish,"* (Esther 4:16). She went against the dictates of her flesh and saved a nation.

Using the <u>law</u>, the Pharisees' flesh told the people that it was unlawful to heal on the Sabbath: *"And the ruler of the synagogue answered with indignation, because that Jesus had healed on the sabbath day, and said unto the people, There are six days in which men ought to work: in them therefore come and be healed, and not on the sabbath day,"* (Luke 13:14).

With Peter, the flesh used <u>doubt</u>: *"Now when he had left speaking, he said unto Simon, Launch out into the deep, and let down your nets for a draught. And Simon answering said unto him, Master, we have toiled all the night, and have taken nothing: nevertheless at thy word I will let down the net. And when they had this done, they inclosed a great multitude of fishes: and their net brake,"* (Luke 5:4-6). Doubt tried to steal Peter's net-breaking load of fish.

The flesh tried to steal the faith of Andrew, one of the disciplines, when he found a lad with five loaves of bread and two small fish. His flesh, using <u>sight</u>, said: *"There is a lad here, which hath five barley loaves, and two small fishes: <u>but what are they among so many</u>,"* (John 6:9). Yet, God used the lad's meal to feed thousands.

42

The man at the pool at Bethesda had been there thirty-eight years, because his flesh told him that he <u>needed help</u> to get into the pool, when the water was troubled: *"The impotent man answered him, Sir, I have no man, when the water is troubled, to put me into the pool: but while I am coming, another steppeth down before me. Jesus saith unto him Rise, take up thy bed, and walk. And immediately the man was made whole, and took up his bed, and walked..."* (John 5:7-9). He didn't need to get into the pool, at all. And of course, Gedaliah's flesh told him that Ishmael would do him no harm. His flesh set him up to be killed.

### You are not Your Flesh!

Although we are admonished to *take no thought;* saying it, we find ourselves, when under pressure, saying whatever thought comes into our minds. These thoughts cause us to oppose ourselves by speaking words of unbelief. Even though they cause us to be weary and faint in our minds, we continue to believe the thoughts, and speak them. Yet, even infants spit out food that's undesirable to them. Isaiah 42:19-20 says: *"Who is blind, but my servant? .... Seeing many things, but observe not..."*

When Jesus healed the blind man, his eyes, as well as his understanding, had to be addressed: *"After that he put his hands on him; he asked him if he saw ought. And he looked up, and said, I see men as trees, walking. After that he put his hands again upon his eyes, and made him look up: and he was <u>restored</u>, and saw every man clearly,"* (Mark 8:23-25).

When we take thoughts from the flesh, we see naturally, but our understanding is darkened. This blind man's eyes were healed with the first touch, but the second touch <u>restored</u> his soul. His understanding was enlightened, and he saw every man clearly: things made sense to him. Without understanding, we will walk by sight and not by faith; we will see, but not observe. When our sight is hindered by our misperceptions: we will see ourselves as grasshoppers, misperceive men, but <u>not</u> perceive that we are wrestling with the enemy of our soul.

Our soul is <u>restored</u> by receiving still waters. John 15:3 says: *"Now you are clean through the <u>word</u> which I have spoken unto you."* But, you must continue to <u>abide</u> by the still waters.

The flesh is not us; it is an accursed thing in the midst of us. Being proud, it is restless: *"It enlarges its desire as hell, and is as death, and cannot be satisfied,"* (Habakkuk 2:5). And, we cannot stand before our enemies until it is removed (see Joshua 7:13).

### The Many Devices of the Flesh

The flesh has many devices. Just to name a few: It masquerades as the schoolmaster, the law, the froward man, the hireling, the wretched man, and the self. It comes against the mind, the will, the intellect, the imagination, and the emotions; and it even comes as an angel of light. It also specializes in cares, legitimate cares, fears (particularly fear of man), unbelief (its main weapon), and sight (things pertaining to the senses).

In an attack against the <u>will</u>, the flesh masquerades as *your-self* by using the pronoun 'I' in statements such as, "I don't like that", or "I'm scared." Its goal is to get us to return to the original sin of focusing on self.

In an attack against the <u>emotions</u>, the flesh endeavors to divide your house, and a house divided shall not stand. It uses past, current, or future plans, disciplines, or day to day distractions (news, gossip, and images from movies), evoking negative emotions and strife. If you find yourself remembering these distractions, you may have an opportunity to awake the original emotions associated with these situations—both the good and the bad. It also wants you to get weary in well doing, causing you to murmur.

In an attack against the <u>intellect</u>, the flesh attempts to undermine your ability through fear of failure, embarrassment, or ineptness. It feeds on ill spoken words by others, tormenting your mind with images that validate unbelief. In speaking first, the flesh sets up snares (traps) that must be broken. If we fail to resist the thought, it remains as a stumbling block, or as a stronghold and slows our progress.

Because we think in pictures, the flesh uses our <u>imagination</u> to provoke images that are in line with its agenda.

Using <u>pleasant knowledge,</u> the flesh tempts you with a godly desire that opposes a godly need. Here, the flesh is operating from the tree of the knowledge of good and evil (the fruit looked good to Eve, but turned out to be evil). You choose the godly desire and find out later that it was a set-up to get you out of the will of God.

The flesh can't tell you something good to do; and you are able to do it. I needed to check on a relative who had injured herself. While cooking, the thought came reminding me of the desire to call her, but that was not the time. I told myself that I would call her after I finished cooking. Each time I returned to the kitchen, I was reminded of that desire. I eventually did call her, at the appropriate time. The flesh is lawless. It wanted me to take thought for this desire—while cooking. When the knowledge is desirable, but the timing is wrong, it's the flesh attempting to by-pass your faith.

The flesh is the sin nature that lies at the door. It uses <u>desires</u> to try to tempt us, but we must master it. Scripture says: *"Let no man say when he is tempted, I am tempted of God: for God cannot be tempted with evil, neither tempteth he any man: But every man is tempted, when he is drawn away of his own <u>lust,</u> (strong desires) and enticed. Then when lust hath conceived, it bringeth forth sin: and sin, when it is finished, bringeth forth death,"* (James 1:13-15).

The flesh wants to usurp your authority. You want to tithe—a second thought reminds you of an unpaid bill. Where did this second thought come from? It's your flesh bringing <u>legitimate cares</u>.

The flesh wants you to <u>second-guess</u> your decisions: A young lady was on her way to school, from an overnight stay at a friend's house, but wanted to stop at her home first to put on her uniform. A second thought told her that she would be late, but she was already late. When she finally reached her class, she was reprimanded for not only being late, but for also being out of uniform. Later, she said, "I started to go home first, but changed my mind and decided not to." Second guessing is a major tell-tale sign of flesh oppression.

The flesh, <u>as an angel of light</u>, comes as a tempter using scriptures. I was trying to do a fast. God has already given me the strategy for the fast, but I wanted faster results. The flesh said, "You know you could do more than what He says." It was citing a scripture where Paul said: *"Having confidence in thy obedience I wrote unto thee, knowing that thou wilt also do more than I say,"* (Philemon 1:21). I endeavored to follow this thought, but found no grace to do it.

The flesh, as a <u>hireling</u>, sells you to the enemy; his wages are death. It sold Gedaliah to Ishmael. John 10:12-13: *"But he that is an hireling, and not the shepherd, whose own the sheep are not, seeth the wolf coming, and leaveth the sheep, and fleeth: and the wolf catcheth them, and scattereth the sheep. The hireling fleeth, because he is an hireling, and careth not for the sheep."*

As a <u>schoolmaster</u>, the flesh condemns and reprimands. It is quick to tell you that you were wrong and scold you in the process. It also <u>excuses</u> an inappropriate behavior with words such as, "I was angry."

The flesh's <u>attacks on our relationships</u> are manifold: It undermines our confidence in others, steals our peace by ascribing ill will toward them, negatively interprets potential reactions, uses criticism, upbraids their behavior, and gives unfavorable reports. We become defiled by our way of thinking (our inner thoughts). Job 18:7 says: *"His own counsel shall cast him down."* Vain thoughts, vain visions, and vain words; herein lies the hallmark of the flesh. Jesus said in Matthew 26:41: *"The spirit indeed is willing, but the flesh is weak."* It must be watched. Gedaliah's major weakness was his flesh. We are only as strong as our weakest link. If not by-passed, the flesh must be crucified.

## By-Passing the Flesh

**What:** *"O the depth of the riches both of the wisdom and knowledge of God! how unsearchable are his judgments, and his ways past finding out!*
**Why:** *For who hath known the mind of the Lord? or who hath been his counsellor? Or who hath first given to him, and it shall be recompensed unto him again? For of him, and through him, and to him, are all things: to whom be glory forever. Amen.*
**How:** *"I beseech you therefore, brethren, by the mercies of God, that ye present your bodies a living sacrifice, holy, acceptable unto God, which is your reasonable service. And be not conformed to this world: but be ye transformed by the renewing of your mind, that ye may prove what is that good, and acceptable, and perfect, will of God,"* (Romans 11:32-36; 12:1-2).

Romans 11:33, explains how the judgments of God are unsearchable and his ways are past finding out. Here, Paul takes us into the concept of sight versus perception. The woman caught in the very act of adultery in John 8:3-11, according to the law and man's judgment, should have been stoned. But, Jesus rendered mercy to her, following the precept that mercy triumphs over judgment. Jesus saw the same thing that the men who judged her saw with His natural eyes, but with His spiritual eyes, He saw the need to reprove with equity.

Our sight is not the problem, our perception is. To have perception, the eyes of our understanding must be enlightened, so we can see as God sees. Without understanding, we would walk by sight; this process calls for the mind to be renewed. This can only happen as we by-pass the flesh.

Paul picks it up in Romans 12:1-2, and beseeches us <u>*therefore*</u> to present our bodies as a living sacrifice: because the body is the temple of the Holy Spirit, it must be in service to Him; and because His judgments are unsearchable, <u>we must allow the body, under the influence of the spirit, to lead us</u>. That is, obey the prompting of the Holy Spirit. Notice this scripture says, present your body first; then, transform your mind.

You will observe that when the body is attempting to lead, the mind will question its decision. Here the wicked one is coming to steal the word that has been planted in the heart (see Matthew 13:19). Those with good hearts, the Bible says, hear the word and keep it, and bring forth 30, 60, 100 fold return. They are not led by their minds; they keep their flesh under subjection.

When we by-pass the mind (the Bible calls it the fleshly mind in Colossians 2:18), we are then able to prove that good, acceptable, and perfect will of God. I have from time to time found myself rendering judgments on matters with an unrenewed mind, only to find out later they were under God's acceptable will.

Samson was operating under God's acceptable will in seeking a wife among the uncircumcised Philistines. His parents questioned his judgment, but God was using Samson to vex the Philistines: *"But his father and his mother knew not that it was of the Lord, that he sought an occasion against the Philistines: for at that time the Philistines had dominion over Israel,"* (Judges 14:4). Samson killed more at his death than he slew in his life, and because he knew the will of God and acted on it, he received an honorable mention in the book of Hebrews.

Ananias and the other disciples judged Saul of Tarsus, yet God was able, through longsuffering, to turn him into a chosen vessel to bear His name before the Gentiles, kings, and the children of Israel.

Because God's judgments and ways are past finding out, we don't know His heart on all situations, but the spirit does. The point is, the mind can't lead us, it must be renewed.

The other day I was obeying the prompting of my spirit go the drug store to pick up some medicine for my brother. I was challenged by the thought that I should call first, so as to not make a wasted trip. After wrestling with this thought, I obeyed the initial prompting. The medicine was there and the trip was not wasted. The mind said: walk by sight, call first. Its goal is to by-pass faith, keeping us in the sense realm.

## Crucifying the Flesh

*"And they that are Christ's have crucified the flesh with the affections and lusts,"* (Galatians 5:24).

The flesh is a wicked counsellor: *"There is one come out of thee, that imagineth evil against the Lord, a wicked counsellor,"* (Nahum 1:11). It operates in the area of the forbidden for purposes of influence and ultimate destruction. It is crucified <u>defensively</u> by: importunity (persistence), meditation, coming to your own senses, setting your mind on spiritual things, or crying ambush. Offensively, joy is the weapon of choice.

### Stand Your Ground

The flesh is crucified through importunity—where you stand your ground until the enemy retreats. Jesus explained this concept in Luke 11:5-10: *"Which of you shall have a friend, and shall go unto him at midnight, and say unto him, Friend, lend me three loaves; For a friend of mine in his journey is come to me, and I have nothing to set before him? And he <u>from within</u> shall answer and say, Trouble me not: the door is now shut, and my children are with me in bed; I cannot rise and give thee. I say unto you, though he will not rise and give him, because he is his friend, <u>yet because of his importunity</u> he will rise and give him as many as he needeth. And I say unto you, Ask, and it shall be given you; seek, and ye shall find; knock, and it shall be opened unto you. For every one that asketh receiveth; and he that seeketh findeth; and to him that knocketh it shall be opened."*

### Day and Night Meditation

The flesh is crucified through day and night meditation on the word of God. Luke 18:1-8 tells a parable to this end: *"That men are to always pray and not to faint. Saying, there was in a city a judge, which feared not God, neither regarded man: And there was a widow in that city; and she came unto him saying, avenge me of mine adversary. And he would not for a while: but <u>afterward he said within himself</u>, Though I fear not God, nor regard man; yet because this widow troubles me, I will avenge her, <u>lest by her</u>*

*continual coming she weary me. And the Lord said, Hear what the <u>unjust</u> <u>judge</u> said, and shall not God avenge his own elect, which cry <u>day and night</u> unto him, though he bear long with them? I tell you that he will avenge them speedily. Nevertheless, when the Son of man comes, shall he find faith on the earth?"* The principle of continual prayer, either by importunity or by day and night meditation, will crucify the flesh (see Joshua 1:8).

### Come to Your Own Senses

The flesh is crucified as you come to your senses. In the parable of the lost son (Luke 15:11-32), the prodigal son came to himself and spoke to himself, saying: *"How many hired servants of my fathers have bread enough and to spare, and I perish with hunger. I will arise and go to my father, and will say unto him, Father I have sinned against heaven, and before thee. And am no more worthy to be called thy son: make me as one of thy hired servants. And he arose, and came to his father..."* Game over! The prodigal son changed his mind. He put his focus back on his father's house and not on himself. An important point: no one can help a prodigal son; he must come to his own senses.

### Mind the Things of the Spirit

The flesh is crucified when it is no longer justified (when we stop making excuses for ill behavior). In the book of Romans, Paul calls the flesh the wretched man. In Romans 7:18-24, he says: *"For I know that in me (that is, in my flesh,) dwells no good thing: for to will is present with me, but how to perform that which is good I find not... For I delight in the law of God after the inward man. But I see another law in my members, warring against the law of my mind, and bringing me into captivity to the law of sin which is in my members. O wretched man that I am! Who shall deliver me from the body of this death."*

Paul realized that: *"They that are after the flesh do mind the things of the flesh; but they that are after the Spirit the things of the Spirit,"* (Romans 8:5). Keeping our minds on the Spirit, crucifies the flesh.

## The Ambush Strategy

In Esther 5:11-13, wicked Haman, while bragging about the glory of his riches, ends his boasting with the words: *"Yet all this avails me nothing as long as I see Mordecai the Jew sitting at the king's gate."* The implication is that Mordecai is watching and praying. With prayers being the front line of defense against the enemy, Haman knows his kingdom can't stand.

In Joshua chapter 7, the children of Israel could not defeat the little town of Ai because there was sin in the camp. After the sin issue was cleared, Joshua was told by God that they could now go and take that city. He told them to use a strategy where it would appear to the enemy that they were defeated, but in fact, they were advancing. Joshua and his warriors engaged the battle, and the people of Ai assumed the Israelites were losing, but it was an ambush. Joshua took the city and won the battle. The principle is that when it looks like you are losing; it's actually an ambush against the enemy.

We are living in the past tense of God's word. His word says: *"No weapon formed against thee shall prosper,"* (Isaiah 54:17). Since the enemy's weapons can't prosper, it has to be God's ambush. In one verse earlier, God explains, in effect, that He has seen the weapons of the enemy and none in his arsenal will prosper.

While learning the faith walk, don't allow yourself to be intimidated by your own errors of commissions or omissions, where you are being accused of missing God. He has satisfied the demands of the sin issue. God is looking for those who maintain the kingdom of God disposition of: righteousness, peace, and joy in the Holy Ghost. When you miss it, count it joy and cry: Ambush!

## Joy

### The Merry Antidote to the Flesh

**What:** *"My brethren, count it all joy when ye fall into divers temptations;*
**Why:** *Knowing this, that the trying of your faith worketh patience.*
**How:** *But let patience have her perfect work, that ye may be perfect and entire, wanting nothing,"* (James 1:2-4).

Joy is the weapon of choice when crucifying the flesh. It is an offensive weapon; it puts the ball back in your court, and it allows you to access your spiritual powers. Without joy, you have no strength to fight the enemy. You will find yourself faint, yet pursing. When Jonah found himself in the belly of the whale, he found his deliverance in the voice of thanksgiving: *"Then Jonah prayed unto the Lord his God out of the fish's belly, And said, I cried by reason of mine affliction unto the Lord, and he heard me; out of the belly of hell cried I, and thou heardest my voice... When my soul fainted within me I remembered the Lord: and my prayer came in unto thee, into thine holy temple. They that observe lying vanities forsake their own mercy. But I will sacrifice unto thee with the <u>voice of thanksgiving</u>; I will pay that that I have vowed. Salvation is of the Lord. And the Lord spake unto the fish, and it vomited out Jonah upon the dry land,"* (Jonah 2:1-10).

Jonah acknowledges the problem: he had observed lying vanities; a hallmark of the flesh. But he was also aware of what needed to be done to bring about a turnaround—joy. Isaiah 12:3-6 says: *"Therefore with joy shall ye draw water out of the wells of salvation. And in that day shall ye say, Praise the Lord, call upon his name, declare his doings among the people, make mention that his name is exalted. Sing unto the Lord; for he hath done excellent things: this is known in all the earth. Cry out and shout, thou inhabitant of Zion: for great is the Holy One of Israel in the midst of thee."*

Joy is powerful, because it places you in the presence of the Lord: *"Thou wilt shew me the path of life: in thy presence is fulness of joy; at thy right hand there are pleasures for evermore,"* (Psalms 16:11).

Joy is a sign that the captivity has been turned: *"When the Lord turned again the captivity of Zion, we were like them that dream. Then was our mouth filled with laughter, and our tongue with singing: then said they among the heathen, The Lord hath done great things for them. The Lord hath done great things for us; whereof we are glad,"* (Psalms 126:1-3).

On the other hand, our fields become wasted when joy is withered: *"The field is wasted, the land mourneth; for the corn is wasted: the new wine is dried up, the oil languisheth. Be ye ashamed, O ye husbandmen; howl, O ye vinedressers, for the wheat and for the barley; because the harvest of the field is perished. The vine is dried up, and the fig tree languisheth; the pomegranate tree, the palm tree also, and the apple tree, even all the trees of the field, are withered:* <u>*because joy is withered*</u> *away from the sons of men,"* (Joel 1:10-12).

Without joy, you will serve your enemy in murmuring and complaining: *"Because thou servedst not the LORD thy God with joyfulness, and with gladness of heart, for the abundance of all things; Therefore shalt thou serve thine enemies which the LORD shall send against thee, in hunger, and in thirst, and in nakedness, and in want of all things: and he shall put a yoke of iron upon thy neck, until he have destroyed thee,"* (Deuteronomy 28:47-48).

With joy, you have strength to stand against your enemy (see Nehemiah 8:10).

# Flesh Alerts!

An alert is a course of action that consists of: the wisdom of God (**What** the situation is); the understanding of God (**Why** you should do it); and the knowledge of God (**How** to perform the good). These alerts will empower you to avoid the wiles of the enemy. The "Why" of each alert will strengthen you to stand against the counsel of the wicked one. The "How" of each alert positions you to be a hearer and doer of the Word of God. The following alerts will prepare you to fight the good fight of faith when warring against the strong desires of the flesh.

## *Flesh Alert!*

### To Fight Weariness in Well Doing

**What:** *"Be not deceived;*

**Why:** *God is not mocked: for whatsoever a man soweth, that shall he also reap. For he that soweth to his flesh shall of the flesh reap corruption; but he that soweth to the Spirit shall of the Spirit reap life everlasting.*

**How:** *And let us not be weary in well doing: for in due season we shall reap, if we faint not. As we have therefore opportunity, let us do good unto all men, especially unto them who are of the household of faith,"* (Galatians 6:7-10).

**Commentary:** Weariness is a child of the flesh—due season is a child of the spirit.

This alert fights weariness. While staying on course and doing the good, you will from time to time experience thoughts that challenge your endurance. The goal of the flesh is to get you to give up before it is time. It wants you to quit, give up, cave in, or faint. But wisdom says: blessed is he who endures till the end.

## *Flesh Alert!*

### To Fight Unbelief

**What:** *"O ye Corinthians, our mouth is open unto you, our heart is enlarged.*

**Why:** *Ye are not straitened in us, but ye are straitened in your own bowels. Now for a recompence in the same, (I speak as unto my children,) be ye also enlarged.*

**How:** *Be ye not unequally yoked together with unbelievers: for what fellowship hath righteousness with unrighteousness? and what communion hath light with darkness? And what concord hath Christ with Belial? or what part hath he that believeth with an infidel? And what agreement hath the temple of God with idols? for ye are the temple of the living God; as God hath said, I will dwell in them, and walk in them; and I will be their God, and they shall be my people. Wherefore come out from among them, and be ye separate, saith the Lord, and touch not the unclean thing; and I will receive you...,"* (2 Corinthians 6:11-17).

**Commentary:** Being restricted by your emotions yokes you to unbelief.

This alert fights unbelief. The goal of the flesh is to get us to believe something God did not say. Here, the enemy is getting you to bypass your peace and make the decision solely on the basis of feelings; you are fighting <u>thoughts that pull on your emotions</u> rather than from the wisdom of God. When you are led by your feelings, you may be joined to unbelief.

## *Flesh Alert!*

### To Fight Lust

**What:** *"Blessed is the man that endureth temptation:*

**Why:** *for when he is tried, he shall receive the crown of life, which the Lord hath promised to them that love him.*

**How:** *Let no man say when he is tempted, I am tempted of God: for God cannot be tempted with evil, neither tempteth he any man: But every man is tempted, when he is drawn away of his own <u>lust</u>, and enticed. Then when lust hath conceived, it bringeth forth sin: and sin, when it is finished, bringeth forth death Do not err, my beloved brethren. Every good gift and every perfect gift is from above, and cometh down from the Father of lights, with whom is no variableness, neither shadow of turning,"* (James 1:12-17).

**Commentary:** Those that are tested are tempted by the enemy, but rewarded by God.

This alert fights lust. These are <u>thoughts that draw us through desire</u>. They are strong desires that cause a longing in the soul. You will be drawn into unbelief in an attempt to satisfy the desire. The goal of the flesh is to separate you from God; the source of true deliverance. When you resist the enticement, you are rewarded by God.

## *Flesh Alert!*

### To Fight Against the Wretched Man

**What:** *"I find then a law, that, when I would do good, evil is present with me.*

**Why:** *For I delight in the law of God after the inward man: But I see another law in my members, warring against the law of my mind, and bringing me into captivity to the law of sin which is in my members. O <u>wretched man</u> that I am! who shall deliver me from the body of this death?*

**How:** *I thank God through Jesus Christ our Lord. So then with the mind I myself serve the law of God; but with the flesh the law of sin,"*
(Romans 7:21-25).

**Commentary:** The wretched man is hindered when we serve God.

This alert fights the wretched man. <u>These are combative thoughts that war against the will of God</u>. This alert warns against a mind that is not fully persuaded. You are not free to obey the dictates of your spiritual intuitions. Your faith is being opposed; you must contend for the right to obey your faith.

## *Flesh Alert!*

### To Fight Against Making Provision for the Flesh

**What:** *"Love worketh no ill to his neighbour: therefore love is the fulfilling of the law. And that, knowing the time, that now it is high time to awake out of sleep:*

**Why:** *for now is our salvation nearer than when we believed. The night is far spent, the day is at hand:*

**How:** *let us therefore cast off the works of darkness, and let us put on the armour of light. Let us walk honestly, as in the day; not in rioting and drunkenness, not in chambering and wantonness, not in strife and envying. But put ye on the Lord Jesus Christ, and make not provision for the flesh, to fulfil the lusts thereof,"* (Romans 13:10-14).

**Commentary:** The end of your faith walk is near; don't fulfill the lust of the flesh.

This alert fights against making provision for the flesh to fulfill its lust (strong desires). You put on the thoughts by thinking on them; and unless they are cast off, it is a matter of time before you act on them. The lusts of the flesh are thoughts that clothe us in pride. This alert warns against yielding to the presumptive will of the flesh rather than to the wisdom of God.

## *Flesh Alert!*

### To Fight Against Frustrating the Grace of God

**What:** *"I am crucified with Christ: nevertheless I live; yet not I, but Christ liveth in me:*

**Why:** *and the life which I now live in the flesh I live by the faith of the Son of God, who loved me, and gave himself for me.*

**How:** <u>*I do not frustrate the grace of God*</u>: *for if righteousness come by the law, then Christ is dead in vain. O foolish Galatians, who hath bewitched you, that ye should not obey the truth, before whose eyes Jesus Christ hath been evidently set forth, crucified among you? This only would I learn of you, Received ye the Spirit by the works of the law, or by the hearing of faith? Are ye so foolish? Having begun in the Spirit, are ye now made perfect by the flesh,"*
(Galatians 2:20-21; 3:1-3).

**Commentary:** Subjecting the flesh to faith, keeps you from works of the law.

This alert fights against frustrating the grace of God. <u>These are thoughts that draw us to fault-find</u>. You are bewitched when you yield to being righteous by the law. And although this process has caused you problems in the past, you continue to be drawn to the observations of the natural man. Yet, we are saved by grace.

### *Flesh Alert!*

## To Fight Against Condemnation

**What:** *"I thank God through Jesus Christ our Lord. So then with the mind I myself serve the law of God; but with the flesh the law of sin. There is therefore now <u>no condemnation to them which are in Christ Jesus</u>, who walk not after the flesh, but after the Spirit.*

**Why:** *For the law of the Spirit of life in Christ Jesus hath made me free from the law of sin and death. For what the law could not do, in that it was weak through the flesh, God sending his own Son in the likeness of sinful flesh, and for sin, condemned sin in the flesh:*

**How:** *That the righteousness of the law might be fulfilled in us, who walk not after the flesh, but after the Spirit; For they that are after the flesh do mind the things of the flesh; but they that are after the Spirit the things of the Spirit. For to be carnally minded is death; but to be spiritually minded is life and peace,"* (Romans 7:25; 8:1-6).

**Commentary:** Sin is condemned in the flesh, when we walk after the Spirit.

This alerts fights condemnation. It warns against the act of cursing our lives or the lives of others. <u>These are thoughts that draw us to compare our strengths to the weaknesses of others; and, condemn them for not living up to our standards</u>. When we walk in the fruit of the spirit, we cannot be condemned, nor condemn others.

## *Flesh Alert!*

### To Fight Against Sin

**What:** *"Knowing that Christ being raised from the dead dieth no more; death hath no more dominion over him.*

**Why:** *For in that he died, he died unto sin once: but in that he liveth, he liveth unto God. Likewise reckon ye also yourselves to be dead indeed unto sin, but alive unto God through Jesus Christ our Lord.*

**How:** <u>*Let not sin therefore reign in your mortal body,*</u> *that ye should obey it in the lusts thereof. Neither yield ye your members as instruments of unrighteousness unto sin: but yield yourselves unto God, as those that are alive from the dead, and your members as instruments of righteousness unto God. For sin shall not have dominion over you: for ye are not under the law, but under grace. What then? shall we sin, because we are not under the law, but under grace? God forbid. Know ye not, that to whom ye yield yourselves servants to obey, his servants ye are to whom ye obey; whether of sin unto death, or of obedience unto righteousness? But God be thanked, that ye were the servants of sin, but ye have obeyed from the heart that form of doctrine which was delivered you. Being then made free from sin, ye became the servants of righteousness,"* (Romans 6:9-18).

**Commentary:** When we reckon ourselves dead to sin, its dominion dies.

This alert fights against sin having dominion over us. <u>These are thoughts that draw us into serving the sin nature</u>. This alert warns against yielding our members: our tongues, our bodies, our emotions, and our attitudes as instruments of unrighteousness—which leads to death. When we declare ourselves separated unto God, we become servants of righteousness.

## *Flesh Alert!*

## To Fight Against <u>Works</u> of the Flesh

**What:** *"This I say then, Walk in the Spirit, and ye shall not fulfil the lust of the flesh.*

**Why:** *For the flesh lusteth against the Spirit, and the Spirit against the flesh: and these are contrary the one to the other: so that ye cannot do the things that ye would. But if ye be led of the Spirit, ye are not under the law. Now <u>the works of the flesh</u> are manifest, which are these; Adultery, fornication, uncleanness, lasciviousness, Idolatry, witchcraft, hatred, variance, emulations, wrath, strife, seditions, heresies, Envyings, murders, drunkenness, revellings, and such like: of the which I tell you before, as I have also told you in time past, that they which do such things shall not inherit the kingdom of God.*

**How:** *But the fruit of the Spirit is love, joy, peace, longsuffering, gentleness, goodness, faith, Meekness, temperance: against such there is no law. And they that are Christ's have crucified the flesh with the affections and lusts. If we live in the Spirit, let us also walk in the Spirit,"* (Galatians 5:16-25).

**Commentary:** Works of the flesh restrict you, but with the fruit of the Spirit, the sky is the limit.

This alert fights against the works of the flesh. <u>These are thoughts that draw you into the manifested destiny of the flesh: his game plan</u> (where you actually fall into the temptation). Here, the flesh says, "I got them." This alert warns against becoming a servant of the flesh. As you exercise the fruit of the Spirit, you put to death the works of the flesh. Life in the spirit should reflect the fruit of the Spirit.

## *Flesh Alert!*

### To Fight Against Conformity

**What:** *"O the depth of the riches both of the wisdom and knowledge of God! how unsearchable are his judgments, and his ways past finding out! For who hath known the mind of the Lord? or who hath been his counsellor? Or who hath first given to him, and it shall be recompensed unto him again? For of him, and through him, and to him, are all things: to whom be glory forever. Amen.*

**Why:** *I beseech you therefore, brethren, by the mercies of God, that ye present your bodies a living sacrifice, holy, acceptable unto God, which is your reasonable service.*

**How:** *And <u>be not conformed</u> to this world: but be ye transformed by the renewing of your mind, that ye may prove what is that good, and acceptable, and perfect, will of God,"* (Romans 11:33-36; 12:1-2).

**Commentary:** When the body leads, you bypass the flesh and transform the mind.

This alert fights against being conformed to this world's system. <u>These are thoughts that draw you into a course of action that seems right, but ends in destruction</u>. This alert warns against presumptuous sins; acting on knowledge that's void of the wisdom of God. When you allow your body to lead, you by-pass the flesh: the spirit is in control.

## *Flesh Alert!*

## To Fight Against Reproaches (Belittlement)

**What:** *"Not that I speak in respect of want:*

**Why:** *for I have learned, in whatsoever state I am, therewith to be content.*

**How:** *I know both <u>how to be abased</u>, and I know how to abound: everywhere and in all things I am instructed both to be full and to be hungry, both to abound and to suffer need. I can do all things through Christ which strengtheneth me,"* (Philippians 4:11-13).

**Commentary:** Your state of contentment is independent of circumstances.

This alert fights against physical, mental, and emotional reproaches. These are <u>thoughts that draw you out of your peace</u>. They expose idols in the heart that you are joined to; areas where self has not been humbled. It is an attempt to spoil your resting place through a need for approval. This alert warns against loving the praise of man more than the praise of God.

## *Flesh Alert!*

### To Fight Against Loss of Identity

**What:** *"But if our gospel be hid, it is hid to them that are lost:*

**Why:** *In whom the god of this world hath <u>blinded the minds</u> of them which believe not,*

**How:** *lest the light of the glorious gospel of Christ, who is the image of God, should shine unto them,"* (2 Corinthians 4:3-4).

**Commentary:** Unbelief blinds the mind; the gospel of Christ cures it.

This alert fights against the loss of our identity in Christ. <u>These are self-serving and fearful thoughts of unbelief</u>. They are designed to silence the still small voice of God. This alert warns against being hardened through the deceitfulness of sin; things that choke the word making it of none-effect.

## *Flesh Alert!*

### To Fight Against Settling

**What:** *"Cast not away therefore your confidence, which hath great recompence of reward.*

**Why:** *For ye have need of patience, that, after ye have done the will of God, ye might receive the promise. For yet a little while, and he that shall come will come, and will not tarry.*

**How:** *Now the just shall live by faith: but if any <u>man draw back</u>, my soul shall have no pleasure in him. But we are not of them who draw back unto perdition; but of them that believe to the saving of the soul,"* (Hebrews 10:35-39).

**Commentary:** Patience will give you the reward that your faith is seeking.

This alert fights against the temptation to settle. <u>These are thoughts that come against your hope</u>. The flesh will attempt to sabotage your faith by discouraging your hope. It is an attempt to unravel your faith. This alert warns against answering a matter before you have heard it, for faith does not disqualify itself. Patience is required. See it through—only believe.

### *Flesh Alert!*

## To Fight Against Not Mixing the Word with Faith

**What:** *"Let us therefore fear,*

**Why:** *lest, a promise being left us of entering into his rest, any of you should seem to come short of it. For unto us was the gospel preached, as well as unto them: but the word preached did not profit them, <u>not being mixed with faith</u> in them that heard it.*

**How:** *For we which have believed do enter into rest, as he said, As I have sworn in my wrath, if they shall enter into my rest: although the works were finished from the foundation of the world,"* (Hebrews 4:1-3).

**Commentary:** It's already done; your faith turns the promise into a rest.

This alert fights against missing promises that were ordained for you before the foundation of the world. <u>There are thoughts that give the opportunity to fear</u>. But, no fear is as weighty as not receiving what God has promised us. This alert warns against failing to mix the word preached, with faith. There is a promise for your life that awaits your faith. You should fear missing it.

## *Flesh Alert!*

### To Fight Against Fear (Timidity)

**What:** *"Wherefore I put thee in remembrance that thou stir up the gift of God, which is in thee by the putting on of my hands.*

**Why:** *For* <u>*God hath not given us the spirit of fear;*</u> *but of power, and of love, and of a sound mind*

**How***: Be not thou therefore ashamed of the testimony of our Lord, nor of me his prisoner: but be thou partaker of the afflictions of the gospel according to the power of God,"* (2 Timothy 1:6-8).

**Commentary**: When you leverage the fear against the testimony, you win.

This alert fights against fear. It is a light affliction of the gospel. Fear is from the family of pride, with its emphasis on self. <u>These are thoughts that fight against your confidence.</u> This alert warns against allowing yourself to be hindered by the spirit of fear as it searches for fear of: people, places, and things; circumstances, situations, and ideas. Fear has no defense against your authority, your perfect love, or your well-disciplined mind.

## *Flesh Alert!*

### To Fight Against Shame

**What:** *"For I am <u>not ashamed</u> of the gospel of Christ:*

**Why:** *for it is the power of God unto salvation to everyone that believeth; to the Jew first, and also to the Greek.*

**How:** *For therein is the righteousness of God revealed from faith to faith: as it is written, The just shall live by faith,"* (Romans 1:16-17).

**Commentary:** Faith to faith is the route that releases the power of God.

This alert fights against shame. <u>These are thoughts that come against your glory</u>. As an agent of pride, its focus is on self; bringing feelings of embarrassment, guilt, or belittlement. This alert warns against allowing feelings of shame to go un-checked. Shame has to be despised (seen as little or nothing at all). Shame tests your ability to be abased and to abase your flesh—it is humbled by wisdom.

## *Flesh Alert!*

### To Fight Against Neglect of Worship

**What:** *"Let the high praises of God be in their mouth, and a two-edged sword in their hand;*

**Why:** *To execute vengeance upon the heathen, and punishments upon the people; To bind their kings with chains, and their nobles with fetters of iron; To execute upon them the judgment written: this honour have all his saints.*

**How:** *Praise ye the LORD,"* (Psalms 149:6-9).

**Commentary:** The enemy is judged through worship in spirit and truth.

This alert fights against the neglect of worship. These are thoughts that limit your praise. The high praises of God engage the whole spirit, soul, and body in the worship and praise of God. These are praises that usher in the presence of God and exalt Him. This alert differentiates between praises where one delights himself in the Lord (praise with soul and body) as opposed to those that extol Him (praise with spirit, soul, and body). We must worship Him in spirit and in truth.

### *Flesh Alert!*

### To Fight Against the Seen

**What:** *"Knowing that he which raised up the Lord Jesus shall raise up us also by Jesus, and shall present us with you.*

**Why:** *For all things are for your sakes that the abundant grace might through the thanksgiving of many redound to the glory of God.*
*For which cause we faint not; but though our outward man perish, yet the inward man is renewed day by day.*
*For our light affliction, which is but for a moment, worketh for us a far more exceeding and eternal weight of glory;*

**How:** *while we look not at the things which are seen, but at the things which are not seen: for the things which are seen are temporal; but the things which are not seen are eternal,"* (2 Corinthians 4:14-18).

**Commentary:** Our light affliction brings us to the unseen realm of glory.

This alert fights against the day of contradiction. These are thoughts that sow disappointment. This is where, what you see, is different from the promise. This alert says the contradiction is temporal, light, and momentary as long as we keep our focus on Him. It warns against the lack of thanksgiving that causes us to faint.

*VERILY, VERILY,*

*I SAY UNTO YOU,*

*EXCEPT A CORN OF WHEAT*

*FALL INTO THE GROUND AND DIE,*

*IT ABIDETH ALONE:*

*BUT IF IT DIE,*

*IT BRINGETH FORTH MUCH FRUIT*

JOHN 12:24

Chapter 4

## The Fruit of the Spirit

The fruit of the Spirit is the only <u>offence</u> against the flesh. Galatians 5:22-23, says: "But the fruit of the Spirit is love, joy, peace, longsuffering (patience), *gentleness, goodness, faith, meekness, and temperance: against such there is no law."* We are righteous because of Christ, but we walk uprightly when we walk in the fruit of the Spirit; however, we have to locate ourselves in the spirit.

When God took me through several dry runs, if you will, of the anointed life, he would catch me off guard and ask, "What fruit are you in?" Each time I was able to check my heart and give him an upright answer. It was a good feeling to check and identify the fruit I was in at that time. One day, He asked the same question. I was a little confused and I was about to say, "I'm a little …" He said: "That is not a fruit!" I smiled, and immediately realized that I was in patience. So, I responded to Him, "I'm in patience." For perhaps the first time, I got a chance to see how patience felt. I remember staying in this fruit for a long time…even months. Eventually, I passed the patience test. The good heart brings forth fruit with patience (see Luke 8:15).

I remember asking one of my nephews for some of his fried rice. He refused to share with me. Later that week, I was still bothered by the fact that he was so unwilling to share. So, I asked him why that was the case. He said, "You didn't share with me." I responded, "But love, against such, there is no law." His response stayed with me. He said, "I didn't know that—I didn't know that love has no law." In other words, he understood that he could respond in love independent of my behavior toward him.

All nine fruits are independent of circumstances, independent of the laws of the flesh, and independent of the behaviors of others. The fruit of the Spirit enables you to finish your course without limitations. You are not moved by the afflictions of life—you are settled.

The fruit of the Spirit enables us to operate out of our divine nature. Using the fruit of <u>love</u>, Noah's sons covered their father's nakedness; they did not expose his shortcomings. Using the fruit of <u>joy</u>, Nehemiah strengthened the builders. Using the fruit of <u>peace</u>, Moses brought deliverance to the children of Israel. The supernatural fruit of <u>patience</u> brings the supernatural promises of God. Using the fruit of <u>kindness</u>, David brought Mephibosheth to his table for the sake of his friend Jonathan, saying: *"He shall eat at my table, as one of the king's sons,"* (see 2 Samuel 9:7-11). The fruit of <u>goodness</u> satisfies the soul; the fruit of <u>faith</u> pleases God; the fruit of <u>meekness</u> receives the engrafted word of God; and the fruit of <u>temperance</u>, instills self-control.

Individuals operating from the flesh are searching for the fruit of the Spirit. The unlovely person is crying, "Have patience with me and I will pay you all." He owes us love, but he can't pay it right now, because he is in his flesh. Paul's solution to this dilemma was to meet each person on their own level. He said: *"To the weak, I became weak that I may gain the weak; to them that are without the law, as without the law, to them that are under the law, as under the law..."* (see 1 Corinthians 9: 19-23).

If the fruit of the Spirit is not operating in your life, the flesh (your flesh) will dog your trail. It will hire you as Balak tried to hire Balaam to curse the children of God (see Numbers 22:6). Each fruit has a reference to our relationship with God and with man. The first fruit of the Spirit is love; however, in our relationship with one another, God requires us to have <u>unconditional and abounding love</u>.

## Love

Philippians 1:9-11, outlines the course for the fruit of love…

**What:** *"And this I pray that our <u>love would abound</u> yet more and more in knowledge and in all judgment;*

**Why:** *that we may approve things that are excellent; that we may be sincere and without offence till the day of Christ;*

**How:** *being filled with the fruits of righteousness, which are by Jesus Christ, unto the glory and praise of God."*

Abounding love causes us to be filled with fruits of righteousness. In the Bible, Ruth gives us an excellent example of abounding love, in dealing with her mother in law, Naomi. Although Naomi was bitter, Ruth never responded to her according to the flesh. Instead, she allowed her love to abound saying: *"Intreat me not to leave you, or to return from following after you: for whither you goest, I will go; and where you lodgest, I will lodge: thy people shall be my people, and thy God my God,"* (Ruth 1:16). We would all agree that this is love. But, Ruth doesn't stop there; she goes on in the next verse to say: *"Where you diest, will I die, and there will I be buried: the Lord do so to me, and more also, I ought but death part thee and me,"* (Ruth 1:17).

God calls love the more excellent way. There are other ways that seem right, but they lead to death. Ruth allowed her love to abound and reaped a recompense for her work and a full reward. By being in the fruit of love, Ruth was able access mercy, and mercy triumphs over judgment.

Naomi deserved judgment for her negative attitude, but she <u>needed</u> the love that Ruth gave her. This averted the threat of Naomi receiving the fruit of her thoughts as outlined in Jeremiah 6:19: *"Hear O earth: behold, I will bring evil upon this people, <u>even the fruit of their thoughts</u>, because they have not hearkened unto my words, nor to my law, but rejected it."* The fruit of love reversed the curse for Naomi. It spared her from reaping the fruit of bitterness; it covered her sin.

## Joy- *your strength*

Deuteronomy 28:47-48 outlines the course for the fruit of joy...

**What:** *"Because thou servedst not the Lord thy God with joyfulness, and with gladness of heart,*

**Why:** *for the abundance of all things;*

**How:** *therefore shalt thou serve thine enemies which the Lord shall send against thee, in hunger, and in thirst, and in nakedness, and in want of all things: and he shall put a yoke of iron upon thy neck, until he has destroyed thee."*

You can either serve the enemy with mumbling and grumbling, complaining, and singing songs of disappointments, or you can serve God for the abundance of all things.

The story is told in 2 Chronicles 20:1-27, where a great multitude came against the children of Judah, and the Bible said: *"And Jehoshaphat feared, and set himself to seek the Lord, and proclaimed a fast. They received the following message: be not afraid nor dismayed by reason of this great multitude; for the battle is not yours, but God's...you shall not need to fight in this battle: set yourselves, stand ye still, and you shall see the salvation of the Lord... when he had consulted with the people, he appointed singers unto the Lord, and that they should praise the beauty of holiness, as they went out before the army, and to say, Praise the Lord; for his mercy endureth forever. And when they began to sing and praise, the Lord set ambushments against the children of Ammon, Moab, and mount Seir, which were come against Judah; and they were smitten."*

Praise causes God to fight the battle—you shall not need to fight in this battle. Praise confuses the enemy and gives you the victory—God sets ambushments (confusion) against the enemy. God inhabits our praise, and in the presence of God is fullness of joy. Joy brings God on the scene. Joy is your offensive tactic; it's your strength.

## Peace - *it calls for us to be unruffled*

Exodus 14:13-14, outlines the course for the fruit of peace…

**What:** *"And Moses said unto the people, Fear ye not, stand still, and see the salvation of the Lord…*

**Why:** *for the Egyptians whom ye have seen today, ye shall see them again no more forever.*

**How:** *The Lord shall fight for you and ye shall <u>hold your peace</u>."*

God is so faithful, that He always shows us what is happening behind the scenes. In Exodus 14, Moses had delivered the children of Israel out of Egypt. Pharaoh was forced to let them go after the last plague, but as he thought about it, the Bible said that Pharaoh and his servants said: *"Why have we done this, that we have let Israel go from serving us? So he took six hundred chosen chariots, and all the chariots of Egypt, and captains over every one of them…and pursued after the children of Israel. The children of Israel were sore afraid: and cried out unto the Lord."*

This scripture lets us know that the enemy is after our peace. When we keep our peace, he is rendered powerless. When the children of Israel held their peace; indeed, they saw the salvation of the Lord. The Lord overthrew the Egyptians in the midst of the sea. This fruit of the spirit activates the essence of peace: standing still; being unruffled. Attacks against your peace will come from every direction, but you must stand still.

Gideon was called to use the same fruit (standing still) when he fought against the Midianites. The Bible says that they <u>stood</u> every man in his place round about the camp: and all the host ran, and cried, and fled. The fruit of peace is an offensive tactic; it's your supernatural ability to take your stand and claim your victory.

## Longsuffering - *long tempered; patient*

1Timothy 1:15-19, sets the course for the fruit of longsuffering…
**What:** *"This is a faithful saying, and worthy of all acceptation, that Christ Jesus came into the world to save sinners; of whom I am chief.*
**Why:** *Howbeit for this cause I obtained mercy, that in me first Jesus Christ might shew forth all <u>longsuffering</u>, for a pattern to them which should hereafter believe on him to life everlasting. Now unto the King eternal, immortal, invisible, the only wise God, be honour and glory for ever and ever. Amen.*
**How:** *This charge I commit unto thee, son Timothy, according to the prophecies which went before on thee, that thou by them mightest war a good warfare. Holding faith, and a good conscience…"*

This fruit calls for us to be supportive of others. They are in straits by their own emotions; unequally yoked to their own unbelief. Mercy is required. If God had not been longsuffering with Paul, he would not have fulfilled the call of God on his life. Longsuffering turns us from unbelief to faith. It gives the time necessary for obstacles to be removed: due season.

In 1Timothy 1:13-16, Paul talks about his past as a blasphemer, a persecutor, and injurious, but he obtained mercy, because he did it ignorantly in unbelief: *"Howbeit for this cause I obtained mercy, that in me first Jesus Christ might show forth all longsuffering, for a pattern to them which should hereafter believe on him to life everlasting."*

The longsuffering of Jesus toward Paul empowered him to be longsuffering with others; he was able to endure hardness as a good soldier: *"Of the Jews five times received I forty stripes save one. Thrice was I beaten with rods, once was I stoned, thrice I suffered shipwreck, a night and a day I have been in the deep; In journeyings often, in perils of waters, in perils of robbers, in perils by mine own countrymen, in perils by the heathen, in perils in the city, in perils in the wilderness, in perils in the sea, in perils among false brethren; In weariness and painfulness, in watchings often, in hunger and thirst, in fastings often, in cold and nakedness,"*
(2 Corinthians 11:24-27).

## Gentleness – *no little kindness*

Titus 3:2-6, sets the course for the fruit of gentleness…

**What:** *"To speak evil of no man, to be no brawlers, <u>but gentle</u>, showing all meekness unto all men,*

**Why:** *For we ourselves also were sometimes foolish, disobedient, deceived, serving divers lusts and pleasures, living in malice and envy, hateful, and hating one another.*

**How:** *But that after the kindness and love of God our Savior toward man appeared, not by works of righteousness which we have done, but according to his mercy he saved us, by the washing of regeneration, and renewing of the Holy Ghost; Which He shed on us abundantly through Jesus Christ our Saviour."*

1 Thessalonians 2:7-8, describes the Christian as being affectionately desirous; being gentle, even as a nurse cherisheth her children.

The fruit of gentleness gives kindness and the love of God access to a person's heart. Gentleness makes us great. My mother shared the story of going to a government facility and ranting about some indiscretion on their part. The lady behind the desk kept saying, "Yes ma'am, yes ma'am; I see ma'am." My mother said that she kept giving the lady *a piece of her mind.* Although my mother was upset, she was also very intuitive. As she was in the process of reading the riot act, the lady kept responding, with gentleness. All of a sudden, my mother stopped, looked at herself, and apologized profusely. She would later say that the lady's response made her examine herself and change her behavior.

Proverbs says the desire of a man is his kindness. If you can't solve the problem; if you can't lend me a hand, can you at least give your kindness? Kindness releases the work of salvation; it satisfies the soul. In Acts 28:2, Paul said: *"And the barbarous people shewed us no little kindness: for they kindled a fire, and received us every one, because of the present rain, and because of the cold."*

## Goodness - *fills the hungry soul*

Galatians 6:9-10, sets the course for the fruit of goodness...

**What:** *"And let us not be weary in well doing:*

**Why:** *for in due season we shall reap*

**How:** *if we faint not. As we have therefore opportunity, let us <u>do good</u> unto all men, especially unto those who are of the household of faith."*

Doing good is an antidote against fainting in well doing. In 1 Samuel 25, the story is told about a man named Nabal and his wife, Abigail. The woman was of a good understanding and of a beautiful countenance, but the man was churlish and evil in his doings. Because Nabal was a prosperous man, David sent ten young men to inform him of the good deeds that he and his men had done on behalf of Nabal's flock. David, being in need at the time, had his young men ask Nabal if he could share a little provision. Nabal refused to help David, who then became offended and sought revenge.

One of the servants brought the news to Abigail and explained to her that David and his men had been very good to them, being a wall of protection to them both by night and day. Abigail then quickly prepared provisions for them. She met David on the road and explained that she did not know of his prior request. She then asked David to forgive her husband's trespass. She encouraged and complimented him; filling his hungry soul with goodness. David was so grateful for the goodness of Abigail that he told her: *"Blessed be thy advice, and blessed be thou. I have hearkened to your voice."* Her advice filled his hungry soul with goodness.

When Moses told his father-in-law, Jethro, of all that the Lord had done unto Pharaoh and to the Egyptians, of their travail and how the Lord delivered them, Jethro rejoiced for all the goodness, which the Lord had done for Israel. What Moses called deliverance, Jethro called goodness (see (Exodus 18:8-9).

## Faith - *brings the promise*

Ephesians 6:11-18 sets the course for the fruit of faith…

**What:** *"Put on the whole armour of God, that you may be able to stand against the wiles of the devil.*

**Why:** *For we wrestle not against flesh and blood, but against principalities, against powers, against the rulers of the darkness of this world, against spiritual wickedness in high places.*

**How:** *Wherefore take unto you the whole armour of God, that you may be able to withstand in the evil day, and having done all, to stand. Stand therefore, having your loins girt about with truth, and having on the breastplate of righteousness; and your feet shod with the preparation of the gospel of peace; Above all, taking the shield of faith, wherewith you shall be able to quench all the fiery darts of the wicked. And take the helmet of salvation, and the sword of the spirit, which is the word of God: Praying always with all prayer and supplication in the spirit, and watching thereunto with all perseverance and supplication for all saints;"*

In 2 Kings 3:21-24, the kings of Israel were preparing to fight the enemy, but they lacked water for their host and cattle. They enquired of the Lord and received the promise of water. The enemy put on his armour, stood in the border, and that morning saw water on Israel's side as red as blood. They said: *"This is blood: the kings have surely slain and smitten one another: …And when they came to camp of Israel, the Israelites rose up and smote the Moabites, so that they fled…"* The enemy saw blood, but the children of God saw the promise: the water that was necessary to defeat the enemy. Israel was able to defeat the enemy, because they put their faith in the promise.

Our faith in the promises is released through prayer and supplication in the spirit. Having on our amour of God, we are able to stand against the wiles of the enemy, and as we pray in the Holy Ghost, we are able to quench all the fiery darts of the wicked. Faith in the word of God will cause you to see the promise and plunge the enemy to defeat.

## Meekness - *reprove with equity*

Galatians 6:1-2 sets the course for the fruit of meekness…
**What:** *"Brethren, if a man be overtaken in a fault, ye which are spiritual, restore such an one in the spirit of <u>meekness</u>;*
**Why:** *considering thyself, lest you also be tempted*
**How:** *Bear you one another's burden and so fulfill the law of Christ."*

God has reserved the task of restoring those overtaken in a fault, only for those that are operating in the spirit. Those who have fallen, often have hidden motives: they are harboring a snare of the enemy: doubt, unbelief, or fear. They are bearing a sin burden and allowing it to reign in their hearts. Restoration by those walking in the Spirit either through prayer or edification is required. Those walking after the flesh would add wood to the fire. The meek would not.

When Miriam and Aaron, spoke against Moses, the words from their mouths were: *"Hath the Lord indeed spoken only by Moses? hath he not spoken also by us? And the Lord heard it,"* (Numbers 12:2). However, the words they spoke did not reveal the real reason for their indignation against Moses. The Bible said they were actually offended because of the Ethiopian woman that Moses had married. Their perceived offense caused them to carry the burden of condemnation. By condemning Moses, they condemned themselves, and without restoration, punishment awaited.

God, knowing the thoughts and intents of their hearts, addressed their hearts. He chastised both Miriam and Aaron, but Miriam was also struck with leprosy and cast out of the camp. Moses, with a spirit of meekness, cried unto the Lord, saying: *"Heal her now, O God, I beseech thee."* God answered Moses and eventually, Miriam was able to return to the camp, completely healed. Those overtaken with a fault are in need of prayer, or edification; not condemnation. Moses, being very meek, bore Miriam's burden through prayer.

## Temperance - *buffeting the body*

1 Corinthians 9:24-27 sets the course for the fruit of temperance...

**What:** *"Know ye not that they which run in a race run all, but one receives the prize? So run that you may obtain. And everyone that strives for mastery is temperate in all things.*

**Why:** *Now they do it to obtain a corruptible crown; but we an incorruptible*

**How:** *I therefore so run, not as uncertainly; so fight I, not as one that beats the air: But I keep under my body, and bring it into subjection: lest by any means, when I have preached to others, I myself should be a castaway."*

The flesh (body of sin) is put in subjection by temperance: the control of self. The enemy of temperance is intemperance. Temperance is tested by a lack of moderation in our: behavior, speech, attitude, and appetite. It requires an adaptation to all men, for the sake of the gospel. Paul, in expressing his perspective on the subject, states: *"For though I be free from all men, yet have I made myself servant unto all, that I might gain the more. And unto the Jews I became as a Jew, that I might gain the Jews; to them that are under the law, as under the law, that I might gain them that are under the law; To them that are without law, as without law, (being not without law to God, but under the law to Christ,) that I might gain them that are without law. To the weak became I as weak, that I might gain the weak: I am made all things to all men, that I might by all means save some. And this I do for the gospel's sake, that I might be partaker thereof with you,"* (1 Corinthians 9:19-23).

Joseph exercised temperance to ward off the untoward solicitation of Potiphar's wife: *"And it came to pass after these things, that his master's wife cast her eyes upon Joseph; and she said, lie with me. But he refused, and said unto his master's wife, Behold, my master wotteth not what is with me in the house, and he hath committed all that he hath to my hand; There is none greater in this house than I; neither hath he kept back anything from me but thee, because thou art his wife: how then can I do this great wickedness, and sin against God? And it came to pass, as she spake to Joseph day by day, that he hearkened not unto her, to lie by her, or to be with her,"* (Genesis 39:7-10).

Daniel exercised temperance to prevent being defiled by unbelief: *"But Daniel purposed in his heart that he would not defile himself with the portion of the king's meat, nor with the wine which he drank...Thus Melzar took away the portion of their meat, and the wine that they should drink; and gave them pulse,"* (Daniel 1:8-16).

Shadrach, Meshach, and Abednego exercised temperance in refusing to serve other gods and worship the golden image that Nebuchadnezzar set up — at the end of their trial, they were promoted.

Jesus operated in temperance, even as a child, when he subjected himself to his parents. Knowing that He should be about His Father's business, He denied himself in order to meet them on their level: *"And when they saw him, they were amazed: and his mother said unto him, Son, why hast thou thus dealt with us? behold, thy father and I have sought thee sorrowing. And he said unto them, How is it that ye sought me? wist ye not that I must be about my Father's business? And they understood not the saying which he spake unto them. And he went down with them, and came to Nazareth, and was subject unto them: but his mother kept all these sayings in her heart,"* (Luke 2:48-51).

Naaman (captain of the Syrian army) tempered his anger and unbelief and received a healing (see 2 Kings 5:10-14).

Peter tempered his doubt to bring the gentiles to Christ: *"Arise therefore, and get thee down, and go with them, doubting nothing: for I have sent them,"* (Acts 10:20).

Temperance places both restraints and constraints on the flesh: "Yes, you will exercise. No, you will not have seconds." It focuses on having a well-disciplined body, stemming from a well-disciplined mind. It refuses to be under the dictates of the flesh. It calls for a dedication to the righteous cause, and to your divine destiny.

## The Fruitful Soul...

### Is known by its devotion to:

**Love:** *"And thou shalt love the LORD thy God with all thine heart, and with all thy soul, and with all thy might,"* (Deuteronomy 6:5).

**Joy:** *"Ye rejoice with joy unspeakable and full of glory: Receiving the end of your faith, even the salvation of your souls,"* (1 Peter 1:8-9).

**Peace:** *"He hath delivered my soul in peace from the battle that was against me: for there were many with me,"* (Psalms 55:18).

**Longsuffering (patience):** *"In your patience possess ye your souls,"* (Luke 21:19).

**Gentleness:** *"The merciful man doeth good to his own soul: but he that is cruel troubleth his own flesh,"* (Proverbs 11:17).

**Goodness:** *"For he satisfieth the longing soul, and filleth the hungry soul with goodness,"* (Psalms 107:8-9).

**Faith:** *"As the cold of snow in the time of harvest, so is a faithful messenger to them that send him: for he refreshes the soul of his masters,"* (Proverbs 25:13).

**Meekness:** *"Receive with meekness the engrafted word, which is able to save your souls,"* (James 1:21).

**Temperance:** *"Therefore will I divide him a portion with the great, and he shall divide the spoil with the strong; because he hath poured out his soul unto death,"* (Isaiah 53:12).

## Power of the Fruit of the Spirit-Summary

Although the flesh fights to uphold the 'Self' through thoughts, ideas, and suggestions, it is dominated by the powerful presence of each fruit of the Spirit:

The Fruit of Love:  Covers *Self*

The Fruit of Joy:  Turns *Self*

The Fruit of Peace:   Silences *Self*

The Fruit of Longsuffering: Restrains and constrains *Self*

The Fruit of Gentleness:   Abases *Self*

The Fruit of Goodness: Subdues *Self*

The Fruit of Faith: Overcomes *Self*

The Fruit of Meekness: Disarms *Self*

The Fruit of Temperance: Controls *Self*

# Chapter 5

## Prescriptions for Life

Prescriptions for life are a group of commandments out of which principles for living have been gleaned. When adhered to, they will bring peace and position us to live the anointed life. God says that we keep the commandments so that we may *be strong, and go in and possess the land.* That land is our souls.

One Greek word for commandment is prescription. The word prescription is a lot more palatable in today's society than the word, commandment. We are aware of the need for prescriptions; when taken correctly, we receive the benefits of the medicine. It is a funny thing about medicine; no one has to tell it what to do. Likewise, the word of God has similar qualities; when it is spoken; it knows exactly what to do. By using the word prescription, God is telling us to live a prescribed lifestyle. After all, Proverbs says that God's words are: *"Life unto those that find them and <u>health</u> for all their flesh,"* (Proverbs 4:22).

The Rechabites are an example of a family that lived a prescribed life style. God commanded Jeremiah to set before the sons of the house of the Rechabites, pots full of wine and cups and to say unto them: *"Drink wine."* And Jeremiah did. *"But they said, we will drink no wine: for Jonadab the son of Rechab our father commanded us, saying, you shall drink no wine, neither you, nor your sons forever... Thus have we obeyed our father in all that he hath charged us, to drink no wine all our days, we, our wives, our sons, nor our daughters,"* (Jeremiah 35).

God commended this family and used them as an example to Judah and the inhabitants of Jerusalem, saying: *"The words of Jonadab the son of Rechab, that he commanded his sons not to drink wine, are performed; for unto this day they drink none, but obey their father's commandment,"* (Jeremiah 35). As the Rechabites were obedient in obeying the commandment of their natural father, our heavenly Father deserves greater honor, not for His benefit, but for the welfare of our souls.

### No Rest for the Soul

After salvation, all the enemies have not been expelled off our land. Our spirits have been saved, but our souls have no rest. Only the engrafted word of God can save our souls (see James 1).

Having no rest, the soul is vulnerable. To the unsaved soul, the enemy says: *"Bow down, that we may go over: and we lay our bodies as the ground, and as the street, to them that went over,"* (Isaiah 51:23). The unsaved soul obeys the dictates of the flesh.

When Joshua and the children of Israel were taking the promise land, the Bible says that they were not able to expel certain enemies (see Judges 1:21; 27; 29; 30; 33-34).

*"The children of Benjamin did not drive out the Jebusites that inhabited Jerusalem; but the Jebusites dwell with the children in Jerusalem unto this day."*

*"Neither did Manasseh drive out the inhabitants of Beth-shean and her towns, nor Taanach and her towns, nor the inhabitants of Ibleam and her towns, nor the inhabitants of Megiddo and her towns; but the Canaanites would dwell in that land."*

*"Neither did Ephraim drive out the Canaanites that dwelt in Gezer; but the Canaanites dwelt in Gezer among them."*

*"Neither did Zebulon drive out the inhabitants of Kitron, nor the inhabitants of Nahalol; but the Canaanites dwelt among them and became tributaries."*

*"Neither did Naphtali... And the Amorites forced the children of Dan into the mountains: for they would not suffer them to come down to the valley."*

Psalm 106:34-42 says: *"They did not destroy the nations, concerning whom the Lord commanded them; but were mingled among the heathen, and learned their works. And they served their idols: which were a snare unto them... therefore was the wrath of the Lord kindled against his people, insomuch that he abhorred his own inheritance. And he gave them into the hand of the heathen; and they that hated them ruled over them. Their enemies also oppressed them, and they were brought into subjection under their hand."*

When the enemy is allowed to stay in the land, we cannot enter the rest of God. Instead of learning of Jesus, we become mingled among the heathen and learn their works. The soul can have no rest until all enemies are driven out.

## Removing the Tares

The prescribed life is a challenged life. Both tares and wheat are found in the same field. Matthew 13:24-30 says: *"While men slept, his enemy came and sowed tares among the wheat and went his way."* You are endeavoring to walk by faith but you are hindered by unbelief, doubt, fear, tradition, philosophy, the flesh, and an un-renewed mind. To set the soul free to live the prescribed life, we must follow the directives of Jeremiah 1:10, where God says: *"See, I have this day set you over the nations and over the kingdoms, to root out, to pull down, and to destroy, and to throw down, and to build and to plant."* This is the process whereby tares are removed from the land. The land must be cleared of all contaminated influences before we can build and plant.

### To Root Out

We are called to root out people who are transgressors (those whose counsel is outside the will of God), out of our hearts. Jesus only had three individuals in his inner circle. Allowing transgressors to have access to the counsel of our hearts can be catastrophic.

David had a son whose name was Amnon, who was in love with his half-sister, Tamar. His friend, Jonadab, a cunning man, gave Amnon a plan to get Tamar alone with him. When she arrived, Amnon forced her to lie with him. David was not able to handle the strife and subsequent death that arose after this transgression. Transgressors must be rooted out.

The Bible says God called Abraham <u>alone</u>, and blessed him, and increased him (see Isaiah 51:2). And, after he separated from his nephew, Lot, Abraham's blessing began to flow: *"And the LORD said unto Abram, after that Lot as separated from him, Lift up now thine eyes, and look from the place where thou art northward, and southward, and eastward, and westward: For all the land which thou seest, to thee will I give it, and to thy seed forever. And I will make thy seed as the dust of the earth: so that if a man can number the dust of the earth, then shall thy seed also be numbered,"* (Genesis 13:14-16).

## To Pull Down

Next, we are charged with pulling down strongholds; casting down imaginations and every high thing that exalts itself against the knowledge of God (see Acts 10:10-48). Peter had to deal with strongholds (foundational beliefs contrary to the will of God), when God asked him to preach the gospel to Cornelius and his family: *"And there came a voice to him, Rise, Peter; kill, and eat. But Peter said, Not so, Lord; for I have never eaten anything that is common or unclean. And the voice spake unto him again the second time, What God hath cleansed, that call not thou common."*

To go from glory to glory, *"We need to know the depth of the riches both of the wisdom and knowledge of God!"* says Romans 11:33, *"How unsearchable are his judgments, and his ways past finding out."*

## To Destroy

We are called to destroy the works of the devil, including cares, nets, snares, cords, and bands. These are devices that should be resisted using the word of God. *"Therefore the children of Israel could not stand before their enemies, but turned their backs before their enemies, because they were accursed: neither will I be with you any more, except ye destroy the accursed from among you; For Joshua drew not his hand back, wherewith he stretched out the spear, until he had utterly destroyed all the inhabitants* (thoughts that steal our peace) *of Ai,"* (Joshua 7:12; 8:26).

## To Throw Down

We are called to throw down idols in our hearts. In Judges 6:25, Gideon was charged with throwing down his father's altar of Baal. We must throw down things (wicked imaginations) that draw us into this natural world that have nothing to do with our divine destiny. *"For mine Angel shall go before thee, and bring thee in unto the Amorites, and the Hittites, and the Perizzites, and the Canaanites, the Hivites, and the Jebusites: and I will cut them off. Thou shalt not bow down to their gods, nor serve them,* *nor do after their works: but thou shalt utterly overthrow them, and quite break down their <u>images</u>."*

As the wicked images are destroyed, we will then be able to serve God: *"And ye shall serve the Lord your God, and he shall bless thy bread, and thy water; and I will take sickness away from the midst of thee. There shall nothing cast their young, nor be barren, in thy land: the number of thy days I will fulfil. I will send my fear before thee, and will destroy all the people to whom thou shalt come, and I will make all thine enemies turn their backs unto thee,"* (Exodus 23:23-27).

## To Build

We are called to build a defense against the abuse, disgrace, shame, or condemnation from the enemy, based on distress: *"Then said I unto them, Ye see the distress that we are in, how Jerusalem lieth waste, and the gates thereof are burned with fire: come, and let us <u>build up the wall</u> of Jerusalem, that we be no more a reproach. So <u>built</u> we the wall; and all the wall was joined together unto the half thereof: for the people had a mind to work,"* (Nehemiah 2:17; 4:6).

We are also called to edify others: *"<u>Build the old waste places</u>: thou shalt raise up the foundations of many generations; and thou shalt be called, The repairer of the breach, The restorer of paths to dwell in,"* (Isaiah 58:12).

Finally, we are called to build our spirit: *"But ye, beloved, <u>building up yourselves</u> on your most holy faith, praying in the Holy Ghost, Keep yourselves in the love of God, looking for the mercy of our Lord Jesus Christ unto eternal life,"* (Jude 1:20-21).

## To Plant

We are called to plant a garden—fulfill the call of God on our lives—make our realm of influence an Eden. We are called to plant the heavens: *"Let thy will be done on earth as it is in heaven,"* (Matthew 6:10).

We are to minister the wisdom of God to others: *"I have planted, Apollos watered; but God gave the increase. So then neither is he that planteth anything, neither he that watereth; but God that giveth the increase. Now he that planteth and he that watereth are one: and every man shall receive his own reward according to his own labour,"* (1 Corinthians 3:6-8).

We are to uproot the devices of the enemy, and plant them in the sea: *"And the Lord said, If ye had faith as a grain of mustard seed, ye might say unto this sycamine tree, Be thou plucked up by the root, and be thou planted in the sea; and it should obey you,"* (Luke 17:6).

We are to be planted in the house of the Lord to thrive: *"Those that be planted in the house of the Lord shall flourish in the courts of our God. They shall still bring forth fruit in old age; they shall be fat and flourishing,"* (Psalms 92:13-14).

Once planted, we are secure: *"And I will plant them upon their land, and they shall no more be pulled up out of their land which I have given them, saith the LORD thy God,"* (Amos 9:15).

The following precepts allow us to partake of God's divine nature and escape corruption. We have included 'landmark' prescriptions that empower us to stay within our anointing. They frame our life for success when we stay within their boundaries: *"Remove not the ancient landmark, which thy fathers have set,"* (Proverbs 22:28).

## Prescription 1
## Being Willing and Obedience

Living the prescribed life admonishes us to:

**What:** *"Come now, and let us reason together, saith the Lord:*

**Why:** *though your sins be as scarlet, they shall be as white as snow; though they be red like crimson, they shall be as wool.*

**How:** *If ye be <u>willing and obedient</u>, ye shall eat the good of the land: But if ye refuse and rebel, ye shall be devoured with the sword: for the mouth of the Lord hath spoken it,"* (Isaiah 1:18-20).

This prescription involves the <u>attitude of the heart</u>. To be in compliance, we must make heart adjustments. In Isaiah 1:19, God calls for us to be willing and obedient to eat the good of the land. If we refuse and rebel, we shall be devoured with the sword.

A young, disgruntled student was sharing with me the reason why she had a bad attitude about coming to class. She said that she was only in class because her mother told her to come. I explained to her that she did not qualify to be blessed. Although she was obeying her mother, the prescription was two-fold, and she must be willing <u>and</u> obedient to eat the good of the land. I showed her the scripture and she immediately adjusted her heart, got into compliance, and is wearing the blessing of that change even to this day.

We are often fooled by the flesh into thinking that we are following the prescribed dictates; however, we have an unwilling heart. We see ourselves as sacrificing, not realizing we must be both willing and obedient. Being willing and obedient also means doing what God says, the way God says it.

The Bible tells the story of Gideon in Judges 6, when he was called to fight the Midianites. Initially, he was able to recruit 33,000 men. They were obedient to show up, but some were full of fear and hesitant about fighting; therefore, they were allowed to return to their homes, and Gideon was left with 10,000 men. God tried them—giving them all the same instruction—lap the water like a dog. Only three hundred were willing and obedient to do it God's way (all the rest of the men bowed down on their knees to drink water). Those that bowed had only the <u>form</u> of Godliness. They were obedient, but theirs hearts were not with God. Gideon, left with only three hundred men, defeated the Midianites and ate the good of the land. God is looking for those of us who are willing and obedient.

Once, after doing my devotion, God gave me specific details on how to make my quota of sales for that day. I proceeded to follow His instructions, but became tempted to make just a slight change. Shortly into the change I began to see the consequences of such an action. I got back on track and made record sales for that day.

**The landmarks for this prescription range from:**

- Being willing and obedient (see Isaiah 1:19).
- Being obedient to the faith (see Romans 1:5).
- To obey is better than sacrifice (see1 Samuel 15:22).
- Though he were a Son, yet learned he obedience by the things which he suffered (see Hebrews 5:8).

## Prescription 2
## Taking Every Thought Captive

Living the prescribed life admonishes us to:

**What:** *"For though we walk in the flesh, we do not war after the flesh:*
**Why:** *(For the weapons of our warfare are not carnal, but mighty through God to the pulling down of strong holds ;)*
**How:** *Casting down imaginations, and every high thing that exalteth itself against the knowledge of God, and <u>bringing into captivity every thought</u> to the obedience of Christ,"* (2 Corinthians 10:3-5).

This prescription involves being a steward over our thought life. Numbers 33:55-56 describes <u>thoughts</u> as inhabitants. It explains the reason why each thought must be taken captive: *"But if you will not drive out the inhabitants of the land from before you; then it shall come to pass, that those which you let remain of them shall be pricks in your eyes, and thorns in your sides, and shall vex you in the land wherein you dwell. Moreover it shall come to pass, that I shall do unto you, as I thought to do unto them."*

The flesh is the dwelling place of the inhabitants that must be dispossessed. It is there opposing all of our good efforts and waging a subtle and almost imperceptible battle, leading us to a place that seems right but leads to destruction. When an instruction is received, or when God's word is sown, the enemy tries to steal it. If he succeeds, you serve him as a servant of unrighteousness.

I was instructed to secure a 501c3. It is a tax filing recognition for a non-profit organization. Although my husband and I had been owners of a non-profit organization for years, I was convinced that I did not have the qualifications to complete this task; moreover, I didn't know anyone else who could do it. I even tried the first time and it was denied.  But, I still felt the Holy Spirit prompting me to do it. Finally, I called a lawyer. He responded very astutely saying, "If I file it for you, you will still have to give me all the information."  Well, that defeated my purpose. I thought, *if I have to give you all the information, then I can do it myself.* The Holy Spirit then gave me a scripture out of Joshua, about my being *slack to possess the land.* Soon after, I started the process of completing the filing. I did such an excellent job, that I knew it would be approved without delay, and it was. A task that I couldn't do a month earlier, I did with excellence a month later and saved the lawyer fees.

There were inhabitants on my land telling me that I could not do it. I believed my thoughts and bought into the image that I needed help. Once I dispossessed the inhabitants, I possessed the land. The day that I mailed the form to the governmental office, the Holy Spirit said: "The sky is the limit."

Because I didn't initially take captive every thought, I bought into the image the flesh sold me; that I could not conquer this task. Proverbs 23:23, admonishes us to: *"Buy the truth and sell it* not; *buy wisdom, understanding, and instruction."* I bought the lie that you had to know taxes to file that type of form; when, in fact, you just had to know how to read and follow instructions.

**The landmarks for this prescription range from:**

- Bring into captivity every thought to the obedience of Christ (see 2 Corinthians 10:5).
- The thoughts of the righteous are right (see Proverbs 12:5).
- Take no thought for your life (see Matthew 6:25).
- Take no thought for tomorrow (see Matthew 6:34).

## Prescription 3
## Say the Same Thing

Living the prescribed life admonishes us to:

**What:** *"I said, I will <u>take heed to my ways</u>*

**Why:** *That I sin not with my tongue:*

**How:** *I will keep my mouth with a bridle, while the wicked is before me,"* (Psalms 39:1).

Sometimes we find ourselves in situations where we are endeavoring to communicate our faith, but in the process, we are challenged by others. We have answered the individual, but the person keeps coming back. Nehemiah shares <u>his</u> encounter in chapter 6:1-4: *"Sanballat, and Tobiah, and the rest of our enemies, heard that I had builded the wall, and that there was no breach left therein; (though at that time I had not set up the doors upon the gates ;) That Sanballat and Geshem sent unto me, saying, Come, let us meet together in some one of the villages in the plain on Ono. But they thought to do me mischief. And I sent messengers, unto them, saying, I am doing a great work, so <u>that I cannot come down</u>: why should the work cease, while I leave it, and come down to you? Yet they sent unto me four times after this sort; and <u>I answered them after the same manner</u>."*

This was an invitation to go into the flesh: *come down.* This prescription requires us to hold the beginning of our confidence steadfast to the end. Don't change your confession of faith. Stay in your wise house.

I recall working with a young lady who was in a very difficult personal situation. She had even given up her baby in the process, which was most grievous to her. First, we discussed the Nehemiah prescription. In our next session she reported, "I had to fight those thoughts eight times before they left me." Both her peace and her baby were returned to her.

**The landmarks for this prescription range from:**

- Answer them after the same manner (see Nehemiah 6:4).
- A man has joy by the answer of his mouth. A word spoken in due season, how good it is (see Proverbs 15:23).
- The heart of the righteous studieth to answer (see Proverbs 15:28).
- I will speak, that I may be refreshed: I will open my lips and answer (see Job 32:20).

## Prescription 4

## Forgiveness

Living the prescribed life admonishes us to:
**What:** *"Sufficient to such a man is this punishment, which was inflicted of many.*
**Why:** *So that contrariwise ye ought rather to <u>forgive</u> him, and comfort him, lest perhaps such a one should be swallowed up with overmuch sorrow.*
**How:** *Wherefore I beseech you that ye would confirm your love toward him,"* (2 Corinthians 2:6-8).

I was talking with a young lady who had a myriad of problems. I was stymied, because I didn't know which problem to address first. The Holy Spirit then spoke to me and said, "Deal with the un-forgiveness, first."

I love the way Joseph handled unforgiveness. When Joseph's brothers stripped him, threw him into a pit, and decided later to sell him into slavery; his response, after his father died, offers us a viable prescription. Genesis 50:15-19 says: *"And when Joseph's brethren saw that their father was dead, they said, Joseph will peradventure hate us, and will certainly requite us all the evil which we did unto him. And they sent a messenger unto Joseph, saying, Thy father did command before he died, saying, So shall ye say unto Joseph, Forgive, I pray thee now, the trespass of thy brethren, and their sin; for they did unto thee evil: and now, we pray thee, forgive the trespass of the servants of the God of thy father. And Joseph wept when they spake unto him. And his brethren also went and fell down before his face; and they said, Behold, we be thy servants. And Joseph said unto them, Fear not: for am I in the <u>place</u> of God?"*

Joseph's use of the word 'place' connects us directly to another prescription from Proverbs 27:8; which says: *"As a bird that wandereth from her nest, so is a man that wandereth from his <u>place</u>."* Joseph affirmed that it was God's place, not his, to deal with his brothers. His place was to forgive, and confirm his love toward them.

Walking in forgiveness requires us to not lay our hands on the prey (individuals used by the enemy). Those individuals who are influenced by the flesh don't realize that they are being used as instruments of unrighteousness. In fighting the true enemy, Queen Esther reported that they did not lay their hands on the prey: *"But the other Jews that were in the king's provinces gathered themselves together, and stood for their lives, and had rest from their enemies, and slew of their foes seventy and five thousand, but they laid not their hands on the prey,"* (Esther 9:16).

Walking in forgiveness requires us to spare the unrighteous on behalf of their righteous nature, because their spirit is blood bought. Here, the old adage: don't throw the baby away with the bath water, applies. Biblically, we say: It not right to destroy the righteous with the wicked (see Genesis 18). The New Testament says: know no man after the flesh (see 2 Corinthians 5). We are to commend them all in unbelief so that we may have mercy on them all. After all, to forgive a Saul is to forgive a future Paul. When we forgive, we *"heap coal of fire"* on their unrighteous nature and receive glory from God for overlooking a transgression (see Proverbs 19:11).

Finally, God said: *"Love your enemies."* Joseph told his brothers: *"But as for you, You thought evil against me, but God meant it unto good…Now therefore fear ye not: I will nourish you, and your little ones. And he comforted them, and spake kindly unto them,"* (Genesis 50:20-21). Joseph did not lay his hands on the prey.

**The landmarks for this prescription range from:**
- I beseech you that ye would confirm your love toward him (see 2 Corinthians 2:8).
- If you will not forgive, neither will thy Father in heaven forgive your trespasses (see Mark 11:26).
- Forgive our debts, as we forgive our debtors (see Mathew 6:12).
- It is not that you didn't do anything wrong, I'm just not holding it against you (Author).

## Prescription 5
## Cast Your Care

Living the prescribed life admonishes us to:

**What:** *"Likewise you younger, submit yourselves unto the elder. Yea, all of you be subject one to another, and be clothed with humility*

**Why:** *for God resists the proud, and gives grace to the humble.*

**How:** *Humble yourselves therefore under the mighty hand of God, that he may exalt you in due time: <u>Casting all of your care</u> upon Him, for he cares for you.*

*Be sober, be vigilant; because your adversary the devil, as a roaring lion. Walks about seeking who, he may devour, whom resist steadfast in the faith, knowing that the same afflictions are accomplished in your brethren that are in the world,"* (1 Peter 5:5-9).

Care is the pressure that underlines a problem. It is not the problem itself. The devil, our adversary, is looking for those who are proud (those with cares). These are the only ones he can devour. Jesus said the devil comes, but will find nothing in Him. No pride will be found and so, no cares. Cares of this world lead us into our foolish house.

I remember taking this prescription for the first time. I was doing my morning devotions when I was interrupted by a legitimate care. At the time, I sold health insurance to small businesses. While finalizing a sale, I forgot to get a second signature. I returned to get the signature, but the business owner was never in. I tried several times and could not reach her. So, the cares started to come: *You still haven't gotten that signature, that lady thinks she is covered, she might be in the hospital, and you could lose your license.* For several days, after my morning devotions, I would jump up and drive to the lady's shop to try to complete the transaction, but she was still not there.

Then, one day I heard someone preach on the subject of casting all of your care on Him. Being a hearer and doer of the word, I followed the prescription exactly. I said, "Father this is a care. I care about the lady's coverage, I care about losing my license, and I care about keeping my job. So, in obedience to your word, I cast the whole of my care on you. I give your praise and I thank you for handling this problem for me...I am now care-free." The next day, during my devotion time, the same thoughts came back to me saying, *God has not done anything about this problem. The lady thinks she is covered, you could still lose your job, she is probably in the hospital, and you could still lose your license.* I was happy to answer my accusers this time. I responded with, "Yes, but that not my problem anymore. That's God's job. My job is to keep my peace."

The same thoughts returned for two more days and I responded the same, only now I was getting stronger. Then the thoughts left. One day I found myself driving early in the morning and I noticed that I was in the lady's vicinity. I thought, *Is this God taking care of the problem?* I noticed a parking space, which was a rare thing, in that neighborhood. I thought, *Let me see if this is God taking care of the problem.* So, I parked, got out of the car, and knocked on the door. When there was no answer, the thought said, *No one is here,* but I knocked again anyway and saw a silhouette of a person. I knocked a little harder and the lady came to the door; and I told her the situation. It turned out that she had been on vacation. We corrected her paperwork and I got a larger sale than the previous one.

**The landmarks for this prescription range from:**

- The lot is cast into the lap, but the whole disposing of it is the Lord (see Proverbs 16:33).
- Cast not away thy confidence, it has great recompense of reward (see Hebrews 10:35).
- Perfect love cast out fear. Fear has torment; he who fears is not made perfect by love (see 1 John 4:18).
- Satan can't cast out Satan (see Mark 3:23-24).

# Prescription 6
## Faith against Such There is no Law

Living the prescribed life admonishes us to:

**What:** *"Examine yourselves*

**Why:** *whether you be in the <u>faith</u>;*

**How:** *prove your own selves,"* (2 Corinthians 13:5).

Galatians 5:22, talks about the fruit of the spirit. It lists them as: love, joy, peace, patience, gentleness, goodness, faith, meekness and temperance. Against such there is no law.

*"Faith is the substance of things hoped for, the evidence of thing not seen,"* (Hebrew 11:1). It is also the substance that is needed to please God. Faith is ultimately what you think. Proverbs 23:7 says: *"As a man thinks in his heart so is he;"* But you can't put faith in a box.

My sister, Betty, told me that she was going to get an apartment and afterwards get a job. I corrected her by saying, "No, first you get a job, and then you get an apartment."

She said, "No, I'm going to get an apartment, and then I'll get a job." I smiled and left her alone. Within a month she had an apartment. Shortly thereafter, she walked around the corner and got a job in her field. I was amazed; faith against such there is no law.

I have used this prescription throughout my life. I find it most useful during times of condemnation, where the flesh is trying to convince me that I did something the wrong way, or that I don't know what I am doing. When you are in faith, there is nothing in the natural that can confirm that you are doing the right thing. The Bible says Abraham went not knowing (see Hebrews 11:8).

The account of the women, who prepared the spices to anoint Jesus' body, is one of my favorite references regarding the use of this prescription. The Bible says they had prepared the spices, and as they were going, they asked among themselves who would remove the stone that guarded the tomb. They kept walking by faith, for there is nothing in the natural that can confirm that you are doing the right thing. When they reached the tomb, they found that the stone had already been rolled away.

Because they used their faith, God gave them a better resurrection. Not only had the stone been rolled away, they were among the first to witness the resurrection. Faith will always give you what you want, or something better. But when you are not fully persuaded, it is an angel of light (enemy). The Bible says Abraham was fully persuaded: *"And being fully persuaded that, what he had promised, he was able also to perform,"* (Romans 4:21).

**The landmarks for this prescription range from:**

- Examine yourself (see 2 Corinthians 13:5).
- Hold fast the profession of your faith without wavering, for He is faithful who promised (see Hebrews 10:23).
- Fight the good fight of faith (see 1 Timothy 6:12).
- The just shall live by faith, if any man draws back my soul shall have no pleasure in him (see Hebrews 10:38).

## Prescription 7

## Swear by Your Own Hurt and Change Not

Living the prescribed life admonishes us to:

**What:** *"If any of you lack wisdom, let him ask of God, that giveth to all men liberally, and upbraideth not;*

**Why:** *and it shall be given him.*

**How:** *But let him ask in faith, nothing wavering. For he that wavereth is like a wave of the sea driven with the wind and tossed. For let not that man think that he shall receive any thing of the Lord. A double minded man is unstable in all his ways,"* (James 1:5-8).

This prescription says we must swear by our own hurt and change not. It addresses our character and matters of the heart. When you give your word, try to keep it. When you say you are going to do something, try to do it. Failure here will cause you to be a double-minded man who, according to the Bible, is unstable in all his ways. A double-minded man is an individual who allows the flesh to change his mind; thus, he is tossed to and fro. When you change your mind based on circumstances, you become unstable. The Bible says: *"Let not that man think he shall receive anything from the Lord."* A wise man, on the other hand, looks well into his going.

The day before my sister's wedding, her maid of honor hung our gowns up in her hotel bathroom to steam them. However, before retiring, she took the gowns from the bathroom and proceeded to go to the closet to hang them up, but changed her mind and decided to hang them underneath the air conditioner, instead. The next morning the dresses were full of soot. When she changed her mind, she became double-minded and disqualified herself from any help from God.

On another occasion, I observed a young man trying to make up his mind about what to eat for lunch. First, he said, "I'll go to Burger

King." Then, he changed his mind and decided to go to another fast food chain. When he picked up his order, he was very dissatisfied, because they had mixed up his order, and the food was not up to par.

You cannot change your mind based on circumstances, but when your desire changes, it is appropriate to change it. I was about to call one of my sisters, but as I picked up the phone, I noticed that my desire had changed. I no longer had a desire to talk to her, but because I had the phone up I called her anyway. She was not in a good mood, and I regretted ever making that call. I thought, *Wow, why didn't I just follow my desire.*

**The landmarks for this prescription range from:**

- He that swears by his own hurt and changes not (see Psalms 15:4).
- Meddle not with them given to change (see Proverbs 24:21).
- Let not your countenance be changed (see Daniel 5:10).
- Let us hold fast the profession of *our* faith without wavering; (for he *is* faithful that promised) (see Hebrews 10:23).

## Prescription 8
## Working the Covenant

Living the prescribed life admonishes us to:

**What:** *"Wherefore remember, that ye being in time past Gentiles in the flesh, who are called Uncircumcision by that which is called the Circumcision in the flesh made by hands;*

**Why:** *That at that time ye were without Christ, being aliens from the commonwealth of Israel, and strangers from the covenants of promise, having no hope, and without God in the world:*

**How:** *But now in Christ Jesus ye who sometimes were far off are made nigh by the blood of Christ,"* (Ephesians 2:11-13).

Because God's covenant of the day and night cannot be broken, when we meditate on His word day and night, God says: *"We shall be like a tree planted by the rivers of water, that bring forth his fruit in his season; his leaf shall not wither and what so ever he does shall prosper,"* (see Psalms 1).

When God told Joshua to take Jericho, he first had to: *"Meditate on the word of God day and night, observe to do all that was therein, then he would make his way prosperous and he would have good success,"* (Joshua 1:8). Night and day meditation is a part of working the covenant.

Years ago I was faced with a huge court case. God had given me a word from the living Bible: *"In that coming day, no weapon formed against you shall prosper,"* (see Isaiah 54:17 LB). That day came and I started meditating on the word of God, but they kept continuing the case month after month. Finally, the Holy Spirit got my attention and said that more word was needed. Although I was still doing my regular morning devotions and praying one hour a day, more word was needed. I realized that I was not meditating day and night. I added the night meditations and within weeks the case was closed. A lady at my church asked God how I won my case. He told her: "She was working her covenant."

Since that time, whenever the odds seemed against me, I would work the covenant of the day and the night. I have found this prescription to work during health challenges as well; victory always followed. Incidentally, I noticed that the accuser of the brethren accuses us before our God day and night (see Revelation 12:10). Even Goliath drew near morning and evening, and presented himself forty days.

Psalm 119:23 says that: *"Princes also did sit and speak against me: but thy servant did meditate in thy statutes."*

### The landmarks for this prescription range from:

- My covenant will I not break, nor alter the thing that is gone out of my lips (see Psalm 89:34).
- By the blood of thy covenant I have sent forth thy prisoners out of the pit wherein is no water (see Zechariah 9:11).
- For the mountains shall depart, and the hills be removed; but my kindness shall not depart from thee, neither shall the covenant of my peace be removed, saith the Lord that hath mercy on thee (see Isaiah 54:10).
- And I, behold, I establish my covenant with you, and with your seed after you (see Genesis 9:9).

## Prescription 9
## He Who Has

Living the prescribed life admonishes us to:

**What:** *"And He said unto them, Take heed what you hear:*

**Why:** *With what measure you mete, it shall be measured to you, and unto you that hear shall more be given*

**How:** *For <u>he that has</u>, to him shall be given: and he that has not, from him shall be taken even that which he has,"* (Mark 4:24-25).

We all go through experiences that challenge our faith. This prescription teaches the importance of holding on to your foundational beliefs, at all costs. Jesus said: *"Simon, Simon, behold, Satan hath desired to have you, that he may sift you as wheat: But I have prayed for thee, that thy faith fail not: and when thou art converted, strengthen thy brethren,"* (Luke 22:31-32). Satan is looking for those who faith can be stolen.

Shortly after having an experience of being sifted, a very distraught young lady approached me. She explained that she wasn't even sure if she was still saved. Nothing had happened on the outside, it was all an inner battle. I told her that it seemed as if she had a belief and that belief had been challenged. She responded, "Yes, that's exactly right." I shared with her Mark 4:25: *"He who has, more will be given, He who has not even from him shall be taken even that which he has."* Without this prescription, things that you thought you were certain about, you will begin to doubt. She needed to contend for the faith. She had to learn to hold the beginning of her confidence steadfast unto the end (see Hebrews 3:14).

It is not enough to have a belief; you must be prepared to fight the good fight of faith. One lady told me that, after God turned her captivity, He gave her pages of scriptures to sustain her faith.

Doubt is a force—a cruel enemy that leads to unbelief. This is where the sifting begins. When Eve was sifted, Satan first planted doubt: *"Did God say, you shall not eat of this tree?"* (See Genesis 3:1-5). Then he planted unbelief: *"God knows the day you eat of it your eyes shall be open; you shall be as gods, knowing good and evil."* Eve, suddenly being aware of her nakedness, lost her identity; then, she became vulnerable to fear. You have to hold the beginning of your confidence steadfast to the end. *He who has, more will be given.*

**The landmarks for this prescription range from:**

- Take heed that no man deceive you (see Matthew 24:4).
- Take heed to your way, that you sin not with your tongue
  (see Psalms 39:1).
- Take heed that the light that be in you is not darkness
  (see Luke 11:35).
- Take heed lest there be in you an evil heart of unbelief
  (see Hebrews 3:12).

# Prescription 10
# Contending for the Faith

Living the prescribed life admonishes us to:

**What:** *"I have fought a good fight,*

**Why:** *I have finished my course,*

**How:** *I have <u>kept the faith</u>,"* (2 Timothy 4:7).

This prescription is akin to a UPS delivery. Once the package is delivered and signed for, it's yours. The book of Jude says: *"We are to contend for the faith that was <u>once</u> delivered to the saints."*

Matthew 13:19 says: *"When the word is sown, the enemy comes immediately to steal the word that was sown in your heart."*

Because the word is a seed, it must be cultivated and harvested; it must be heard and kept. You must protect the seed from weeds and other contaminating influences. To contend means to fight for the word: fight to believe the promises of God and fight to believe that what He says is true. Paul says: *"Fight the good fight of faith,"* (1Timothy 6:12).

The enemy is not after you, he's after your faith, because faith has the ability to: *"Subdue kingdoms, work righteousness, obtain promises, stop the mouths of lions, quench the violence of fire, escape the edge of the sword, out of weakness were made strong, waxed valiant in fight, turn to flight the armies of the aliens,"* (Hebrew 11:33-34). The force of faith cannot be stopped, as God's word cannot return void.

Isaiah 55:11 says: *"So shall my word be that goeth forth out of my mouth: it shall not return unto me void, but it shall accomplish that which I please, and it shall prosper in the thing whereto I sent it."* Because the word will not return void, our only challenge is time.

Seed-time-harvest is the process of transferring the seed (in the heart) into a promise. The time phase is where we will reap if we don't faint, for the harvest has been assigned to a due season. Seed sown in good soil will always reap in due season.

112

In Deuteronomy 2:24-25, God promised the children of Israel land that was possessed by the enemy. He told them to rise up take their journey—he had given into their hand the enemy of that land and his land—begin to possess it and contend with him in battle.

In contending in battle, God said: *"This day will I begin to put the dread of thee and the fear of thee upon the nations that are under the whole heaven, who shall hear report of thee, and shall tremble, and be in anguish because of thee."*

We are commanded to contend and win.

**The landmarks for this prescription range from:**

- Contending for the faith (see Jude 1:3).
- Contending with the enemy, to possess the land (see Deuteronomy 2:24-25).
- Contending with the mountains; speaking to mountains (see Micah 6:1).
- Contending with the wicked (flesh), by keeping the precepts (see Proverbs 28:4).

## Prescription 11
## Set Your Mind on Things Above

Living the prescribed life admonishes us to:

**What:** *"<u>Set your affection on things above</u>, not on things on the earth.*
**Why:** *For ye are dead, and your life is hid with Christ in God. When Christ, who is our life, shall appear, then shall ye also appear with him in glory.*
**How:** *Mortify therefore your members which are upon the earth; fornication, uncleanness, inordinate affection, evil concupiscence, and covetousness, which is idolatry: For which things' sake the wrath of God cometh on the children of disobedience: In the which ye also walked some time, when ye lived in them,"* (Colossians 3:2-7).

This prescription is vitally important. It involves being ready and prepared by setting the atmosphere in your heart. In your home, the thermostat is used to regulate the temperature. Once the thermostat is set, it controls the environment. If the surrounding air changes, you will often check the thermostat to see if it needs adjusting. This prescription is similar. When situations or thoughts attack, you check your setting. What does the word say? Your job is to echo the word.

- The word says: *By His strips I am healed.*
- The word says: *I have favor with God and man.*
- The word says: *No weapon formed against me shall prosper.*
- The word says: *In all things I am more than a conqueror.*
- The word says: *I am the head and not the tail.*

Remember, the word is a seed. You must mix it with faith. You mix the word by speaking it out loud, "By His stripes I am healed." You keep your setting on this 'channel' until the desired temperature is met. You endure to the end.

An unset mind has its own agenda; it's unreliable and cannot be trusted. You don't know if it will follow the prescription or not.

Sometimes it speaks the word, other times it speaks its emotions. It is not faithful during times of testing.

In the Book of Esther, chapter 2:13-17, Esther was competing for the position of queen. Each contestant was: *"Given whatsoever she desired to go with her out of the house of the women unto the king's house."* Esther, the Bible said: *"Required nothing but what Hegai the king's chambermaid, the keeper of the women, appointed. And Esther obtained favor in the sight of all them that looked upon her."* Eventually, the king set the royal crown upon her head. Esther did not have her own agenda. She did not trust her own mind to direct her. The other contestants did and lost.

When the mind is set on things above, we don't have to rethink the decision, and when the mind is set on things above, you cannot be tempted with evil in that area. Temptations come to see if your mind is set; to test if: *"You stand fast in one spirit, with one mind striving together for the faith of the gospel,"* (Philippians 1:27).

### The Landmarks for this prescription range from:

- Setting our affections on thing above, not on things of this earth (see Colossians 3:2).
- Setting our face like a flint, so that we will not be moved (see Isaiah 50:7).
- Setting our affections to the house my God (see 1 Chronicles 29:3).
- Setting our love upon Him, He will deliver us (see Psalms 91:14).

## Prescription 12
## Judge not that you not be Judged

Living the prescribed life admonishes us to:

**What:** *"Judge not, that ye be not judged.*
**Why:** *For with what judgment ye judge, ye shall be judged: and with what measure ye mete, it shall be measured to you again. And why beholdest thou the mote that is in thy brother's eye, but considerest not the beam that is in thine own eye? Or how wilt thou say to thy brother, Let me pull out the mote out of thine eye; and, behold, a beam is in thine own eye?*
**How:** *Thou hypocrite, first cast out the beam out of thine own eye; and then shalt thou see clearly to cast out the mote out of thy brother's eye,"* (Matthew 7:1-5).

This prescription wars against the spirit of condemnation that weakens the spirit and causes sicknesses and many to sleep.

We open ourselves up to condemnation when we judge others. Judging others is a sign of a hungry soul. In 1 Corinthians 11:33-34, Paul exhorts us to eat at home that we come not into condemnation: *"Wherefore, my brethren, when ye come together to eat, tarry one for another. And if any man hunger, let him eat at home; that ye come not together unto condemnation. And the rest will I set in order when I come."*

Paul points out that we are all at different levels of development. When we see a brother or a sister who has not risen to our standard, we need to wait on their growth and development. However, we should not expect to get our needs met from them. We should get our needs met from our own hearts, during our time of devotion, at home. If you feel that people are unlovely, to avoid condemnation, meditate on how much God loves you—get the love you need at home. Before we condemn, we must: *"Take the beam out of our own eye and we shall see clearly how to take the speck out of our brother's eye,"* (Luke 6:41-42).

The cry of those being judged is: have patience with me and I will pay you what I owe; we owe one another love.

**The Landmarks for this prescription range from:**

- Who art thou that judgest another man's servant? To his own master he will stand or fall. Yea, he shall be holden up for God is able to make him stand (see Romans 14:4).
- If we judge ourselves we shall not be judged (see 1 Corinthians 11:31).
- For he shall have judgment without mercy, that has shown no mercy and mercy rejoices against judgment (see James 2:13).
- Judge not, that ye be not judged (see Matthew 7:1).

# Prescription 13
# Warning the Righteous

Living the prescribed life admonishes us to:

**What:** *"Again, when a righteous man doth turn from his <u>righteousness</u>, and commit iniquity, and I lay a stumbling block before him, he shall die:*

**Why:** *because thou hast not given him warning, he shall die in his sin, and his righteousness which he hath done shall not be remembered; but his blood will I require at thine hand.*

**How:** *Nevertheless if thou <u>warn the righteous</u> man, that the righteous sin not, and he doth not sin, he shall surely live, because he is warned; also thou hast delivered thy soul,"* (Ezekiel 3:20-21).

The other day, the Holy Spirit had me recall an incident that occurred the night before. At an event, a young lady was very pleasant—embracing different people, and seemed to have a genuinely happy disposition. You could say she was in her element. A few hours later however, she became involved in a rather heated altercation with her mother. The two of them parted company; both of them offended and seemingly bewildered. After recalling the incident, I acknowledged to the Holy Spirit that I too, was taken aback by the young lady's sudden change in behavior toward her mother. His response to me was: "She has a stumbling block."

Stumbling blocks are idols (misperceptions; pride-filled frames of reference; preconceived ideas; private logic) in a person's heart that causes them to become offended; it is an occasion to fall. If the young lady believes that her mother is <u>always</u> doing this or that, her pride (presumption) will cause her to respond functionally, without love or mercy. The things that we hold against others become ordinances and they cause us to stumble. Although Jesus has taken the ordnances and nailed them to the cross, we continue to hold issues of the flesh against one another—we hold them in the past.

We enter the field of stumbling when our speech testifies against us. We find ourselves using superlatives such as, "She always—you never," and so forth. Either we have forgiven those to whom God has forgiven, or our standards are higher than God's. In any event, we are called to sanctify ourselves and cast out the stumbling block.

When you warn the righteous it yields two winners: he lives and your soul is delivered.

### The Landmarks for this prescription range from:

- Warn the righteous (see Ezekiel 3:21).
- And shall say, Cast ye up, cast ye up, prepare the way, take up the stumbling block out of the way of my people (see Isaiah 57:14).
- Let us not therefore judge one another anymore: but judge this rather, that no man put a stumbling block or an occasion to fall in his brother's way (see Romans 14:13).
- But take heed lest by any means this liberty of yours become a stumbling block to them that are weak (see 1 Corinthians 8:9).

## Prescription 14
## Pride Checklist

Living the prescribed life admonishes us to:

**What:** *"Behold,*

**Why:** *his soul which is <u>lifted up</u> is not <u>upright</u> in him:*

**What:** *but the just shall live by his faith,"* (Habakkuk 2:4).

Pride separates us from God. It is the enemy behind every thought of presumption, doubt, unbelief, and fear. Pride causes us to fall into iniquity; leaving paths of uprightness, and walking in the imagination of the heart. It is an act of self-will. Contention follows it.

In Genesis 34:2, Jacob's daughter, Dinah, was violated by the prince of that country, a young man by the name of Shechem. Two of her brothers, Simeon and Levi, killed Shechem. They felt justified in vindicating her honor because she had been defiled. They presumed that they were correct in their actions. However, their father, Jacob, saw it differently; he called it an act of self-will: *"Simeon and Levi are brethren; instruments of cruelty are in their habitations. O my soul, come not thou into their secret; unto their assembly, mine honour, be not thou united: for in their anger they slew a man, and in their <u>self-will</u> they digged down a wall. Cursed be their <u>anger,</u> for it was fierce; and their wrath, for it was cruel: I will divide them in Jacob, and scatter them in Israel,"* (Genesis 49:5-7).

Jacob realized that God was not in his sons' decision. When the knowledge of God is not in our thoughts we are in pride. When pride is at the helm, the soul continues to operate, but it is not upright. It is void of truth.

The humble, on the other hand, bring <u>the will of self</u> into subjection. They seek the wisdom of God through prayer, not presumption: *"If my people, which are called by my name, shall humble themselves, and pray, and seek my face, and turn from their wicked ways; then will I hear from heaven, and will forgive their sin, and will heal their land.*

*Now mine eyes shall be open, and mine ears attent unto the prayer that is made in this place. For now have I chosen and sanctified this house that my name may be there forever: and mine eyes and mine heart shall be there perpetually,"* (2 Chronicles 7:14-16). When lifted up in pride, the soul falls from faith.

Years ago, three of my sisters were fighting over their stuff—two against one. When I was told about the incident, it grieved me. I said to myself, *they are fighting over stuff.* God corrected me and said: "No they are not. They are fighting because of pride." Later, I learned that: *"Only by pride comes contention,"* (Proverbs 13:10).

The only cause for strife is pride. With pride and strife you have two deadly forces. These forces are not just after the other person; they are after both the host <u>and</u> the prey; the flesh gets two for one. Strife is akin to taking fire into your bosom and thinking that you will not get burned.

In learning how to handle strife in my own life, God gave me a strategy found in Proverbs 26:20, which states: *"Where no wood is, there the fire goes out."* The flesh is a wood vessel. Don't add wood to the fire!

**The Landmarks for this prescription range from:**

- <u>Only by pride cometh contention</u>: but with the well advised *is* wisdom (see Proverbs 13:10).
- <u>Pride *goeth* before destruction</u>, and an haughty spirit before a fall (see Proverbs 16:18).
- The <u>pride of thine heart</u> hath deceived thee, thou that dwellest in the clefts of the rock, whose habitation *is* high; that saith in his heart, who shall bring me down to the ground? (See Obadiah 1:3).
- For all that *is* in the world, the lust of the flesh, and the lust of the eyes, and <u>the pride of life</u>, is not of the Father, but is of the world. And the world passeth away, and the lust thereof: but he that doeth the will of God abideth forever (see 1 John 2:16-17).

## Prescription 15
## Many Waters Can't Quench Love

Living the prescribed life admonishes us to:

**What:** *"Ye have not yet resisted unto blood, striving against sin. And ye have forgotten the exhortation which speaketh unto you as unto children, My son, despise not thou the chastening of the Lord, nor faint when thou art rebuked of him:*

**Why:** *For whom the Lord loveth he chasteneth, and scourgeth every son whom he receiveth.*

**How:** *If ye endure chastening, God dealeth with you as with sons; for what son is he whom the father chasteneth not? But if ye be without chastisement, whereof all are partakers, then are ye bastards, and not sons,"* (Hebrews 12:4-8).

I had a vision of a man who was fearful of losing the love of certain individuals. God showed me that he was limiting the type of information he was giving them. I was assigned to tell this gentleman a scripture from Songs of Songs 8:7, which reads: *"Many waters cannot quench love, neither can the floods drown it."* It was well received.

Many are afraid to tell a loved one the truth, out of fear of losing their love. They would rather see that person maintain a level of immaturity, than challenge him or her, with the Word of God, to come up higher. When we are kept at a level of immaturity, we cannot access our inheritance, and no one wins.

We are called to feed the church of God (those who are called by His name) to edify and exhort. When we fail to declare all the counsel of God to those in need of edifying, their blood is on our hands. In Acts 20:26-27, Paul says: *"Wherefore I take you to record this day that I am pure from the blood of all men. For I have not shunned to declare unto you all the counsel of God."*

I found myself in a situation last summer where edifying was going to be a challenge. I had been working with a relative who refused to come out of the flesh. I spent twenty to thirty minutes debating over an issue that could only benefit him. He finally turned himself and came to his senses. He was so taken aback by the incident that he asked another relative, "What's wrong with her? She's not getting anything out of it!"

In his world, people didn't challenge each other to come up higher. They find themselves either accusing or excusing the individual's behavior saying, "It may be God." But, if it is not good and perfect, it is not God.

When we take the time to reprove individuals, they become clean through the word spoken to them. Instead of losing their love, they gain maturity, and we deliver our souls. The Bible says: *"As an earring of gold, and an ornament of fine gold, so is a wise reprover upon an obedient ear,"* (Proverbs 25:12).

In Acts 20:20, Paul, in effect said, that he did not let his friends drive drunk. In his own words he said: *"And how I kept back nothing that was profitable unto you, but have shewed you, and have taught you publickly, and from house to house."*

**The Landmarks for this prescription range from:**
- Yea, they <u>despised the pleasant land,</u> they believed not his word: But murmured in their tents, and hearkened not unto the voice of the Lord (see Psalms 106:24-25).
- Whoso <u>despiseth the word</u> shall be destroyed: but he that feareth the commandment shall be rewarded (see Proverbs 13:13).
- He therefore that despiseth <u>despiseth not man, but God,</u> who hath also given unto us his Holy Spirit (see 1 Thessalonians 4:8).
- He that refuseth instruction <u>despiseth his own soul</u>: but he that heareth reproof getteth understanding (see Proverbs 15:32).

## Prescription 16
## Anger Finds Its Resting Place

Living the prescribed life admonishes us to:

**What:** *"Let no corrupt communication proceed out of your mouth, but that which is good to the use of edifying,*

**Why:** *that it may minister grace unto the hearers. And grieve not the Holy Spirit of God, whereby ye are sealed unto the day of redemption.*

**How:** *Let all bitterness, <u>and wrath, and anger,</u> and clamour, and evil speaking, be put away from you, with all malice: And be ye kind one to another, tenderhearted, forgiving one another, even as God for Christ's sake hath forgiven you,"* (Ephesians 4:29-32).

I once worked with a gentleman who was very argumentative. In one interview he confessed, "My temper is this quick," and he snapped his fingers, for emphasis. That evening, the Holy Spirit led me to Ecclesiastes 7:9, and told me to share it with the gentleman. I was reluctant, saying, "You want me to call this man a fool?" I tossed and turned all night, but I realized that I had to do it.

In our next session, I told him that I had something to show him. I showed him the verse, which read: *"Be not hasty in thy spirit to be angry: for anger resteth in the bosom of fools,"* (Ecclesiastes 7:9). He looked at it with a sense of amazement and said, "I am nobody's fool!" However, in a later session, he said, "That scripture changed my life. I used to be quick to get angry, but now nothing upsets me. I didn't like being a fool."

Anger does find its resting place in the hearts of fools. It is a fruit of pride that comes from a focus on self. It is a disjunctive emotion that assaults the soul. It not only separates us from God and others, but it is an affront on the spirit as well. Anger is a call from the flesh to do its bidding. The flesh is after the fruit of the spirit, knowing that without fruit, you are unable to operate against him.

Ephesians 4:26-27 admonishes us to: *"Be ye angry, and sin not: let not the sun go down upon your wrath: Neither give place to the devil."* It suggests that there is an anger that leads to sin, because it gives place to the devil. It can be deadly as it releases the enemy into our lives, to bring every evil work (see James 3:16).

Righteous anger is anger that's directed against the enemy: his deceptions, the ills of society, and areas where the enemy has been given a place. It should be used when you are rendering judgment against attacks of the enemy. For even God reserves His wrath for His enemies.

However, when dealing with flesh and blood, God turns the other cheek: *"But he, being full of compassion, forgave their iniquity, and destroyed them not: yea, many a time turned he his anger away, and did not stir up all his wrath. For he remembered that they were but flesh; a wind that passeth away, and cometh not again,"* (Psalms 78:38-39).

## The Landmarks for this prescription range from:

- Cease from anger, and forsake wrath: fret not thyself in any wise to do evil. For evildoers shall be cut off: but those that wait upon the Lord, they shall inherit the earth (see Psalms 37:8-9).
- Wherefore, my beloved brethren, let every man be swift to hear, slow to speak, slow to wrath: For the wrath of man worketh not the righteousness of God (see James 1:19-20).
- He that hath no rule over his own spirit is like a city that is broken down, and without walls (see Proverbs 25:28).
- The discretion of a man deferreth his anger; and it is his glory to pass over a transgression (see Proverbs 19:11).

## Prescription 17
## As a Man Thinks in His Heart

**What:** *"Eat thou not the bread of him that hath an evil eye, neither desire thou his dainty meats:*
**Why:** *For <u>as he thinketh in his heart</u>, so is he: Eat and drink, saith he to thee; but his heart is not with thee. The morsel which thou hast eaten shalt thou vomit up, and lose thy sweet words,"* (Proverbs 23:6-8).

David and Saul give us an excellent example of how this prescription works. Saul, the first king of Israel, was extremely jealous of David. Perceiving that David was the next heir to the throne, he sought to kill him, hoping to keep the kingdom in his lineage. King Saul was relentless in his pursuit to kill David. However, it was David who finally got the opportunity to kill King Saul. We pick up the conversation in 1 Samuel 26:

*"Then said Abishai to David, God hath delivered thine enemy into thine hand this day: now therefore let me smite him, I pray thee, with the spear even to the earth at once, and I will not smite him the second time.*

*And David said to Abishai, Destroy him not: for who can stretch forth his hand against the LORD's anointed, and be guiltless? David said furthermore, As the LORD liveth, the LORD shall smite him; or his day shall come to die; or <u>he shall descend into battle, and perish</u>. The LORD forbid that I should stretch forth mine hand against the LORD's anointed: but, I pray thee, take thou now the spear that is at his bolster, and the cruse of water, and let us go. So David took the spear and the cruse of water from Saul's bolster; and they gat them away, and no man saw it, nor knew it, neither awaked: for they were all asleep; because a deep sleep from the LORD was fallen upon them,"* (1 Samuel 26:1-12).

Then, David awakened Saul and informed him of the opportunity he had to destroy him: *"And Saul knew David's voice, and said, is this thy voice, my son David? And David said, it is my voice, my lord,*

*O king. And he said, wherefore doth my lord thus pursue after his servant? For what have I done? or what evil is in mine hand?...Then said Saul, I have sinned: return, my son David: for I will no more do thee harm, because my soul was precious in thine eyes this day: behold, I have played <u>the fool</u>, and have erred exceedingly... Then Saul said to David, Blessed be thou, my son David: thou shalt both do great things, and also shalt still prevail. So David went on his way, and Saul returned to his place,"* (1 Samuel 26:17-25).

*"<u>And David said in his heart</u>, I shall now perish one day by the hand of Saul: there is nothing better for me than that I should speedily escape into the land of the Philistines; and Saul shall despair of me, to seek me any more in any coast of Israel: so shall I escape out of his hand. And David arose, and he passed over with the six hundred men that were with him unto Achish, the son of Maoch, king of Gath. And David dwelt with Achish at Gath...And it was told Saul that David was fled to Gath: <u>and he sought no more again for him</u>,"* (1 Samuel 27:1-4).

## The words David spoke in his heart:

David perceived that unless he escaped into the land of the Philistines, Saul would continue to pursue. He believed that this maneuver would cause Saul to despair of seeking him anymore, and it did.

## The words David said in his heart came to pass:

When Saul heard that David had fled to Gath, he sought him no more. In 1 Samuel 30, Saul descended in battle, and perished. David did not think, nor speak those things that he did not want to come to pass, during this season of his life. Now, he was able to trust his heart. He refused to allow thoughts that were contrary to the will of God, to enter his heart; had they entered his heart, he would have followed them. Instead, he received thoughts from his heart to delude his pursuer permanently. This thought allowed him to obey the

127

command of God's heart: *"Touch not my anointed, do my prophet no harm,"* (Psalms 105:15).

Saul followed the evil thoughts that were placed in his heart. He *ate and drank* every thought (he thought and acted on it). David, on the other hand, refused to follow thoughts that came to him, but rather followed those thoughts that came <u>through</u> him. David had to distinguish between thoughts coming to him, to steal his peace, versus those coming through him; guiding him to his divine destiny.

The thoughts of our heart manifest themselves in reality. This scripture reveals that the enemy is aware of our spiritual make up—we are designed to operate in concert to the thoughts in our hearts. When this prescription is used in reverse we find ourselves working against our own lives, as we bring to pass the undesirable things in our hearts. Within a few days Saul dies in battle, whereas David lived out his lifetime.

*IN THE AREA OF YOUR ANOINTING,*

*YOUR "LIGHT" IS ALWAYS TURNED ON.*

*OTHERS HAVE TO STUGGLE FOR*

*WHAT YOU HAVE, NATURALLY.*

AUTHOR

# Chapter 6

## The Anointed Life

The Anointed Life is a life lived <u>freely</u> under the influence of the Holy Spirit. As our Comforter, the Holy Spirit guides us with His eye, and into His holy habitation. He satisfies our souls in drought and guides our feet in the way of peace. As the Spirit of Truth, He guides us into all truth and shows us things to come. When tested, He will show us the way of escape. He is the: *"Father of mercies, and the God of all comfort: who comforts us in all our tribulations that we may be able to comfort them which are in any trouble, by the comfort wherewith we ourselves are comforted of God,"* (2 Corinthians 1:3-4).

This life lived through the guidance of the Holy Spirit will bring vengeance, conquest, and comfort. To carry out this work, we have been given the ministry of reconciliation; God has given us the task of reconciling His people to Himself. To accomplish this mission we have been anointed.

## Components of the Anointed Life

The Power of the Anointing

The Purpose of the Anointing

The Anointing Disposition

The Rewards of the Anointing

The Anointing Weapons

# The Power of the Anointing

The anointing ushers in the kingdom within: *"And in the days of these kings shall the God of heaven set up a kingdom, which shall never be destroyed: and the kingdom shall not be left to other people, but it shall break in pieces and consume all these kingdoms, and it shall stand forever,"* (Daniel 2:44).

### The Anointing Ushers in the Day of Vengeance

*"The Spirit of the Lord GOD is upon me; because the Lord hath <u>anointed</u> me to preach good tidings unto the meek; he hath sent me to bind up the brokenhearted, to proclaim liberty to the captives, and the opening of the prison to them that are bound; To proclaim the acceptable year of the Lord, and the day of vengeance of our God; to comfort all that mourn,"* (Isaiah 61:1-2).

### The Anointing Destroys Yokes of Bondage

*"And it shall come to pass in that day, that his burden shall be taken away from off thy shoulder, and his yoke from off thy neck and the yoke shall be destroyed because of the <u>anointing</u>,"* (Isaiah 10:27).

### The Anointing Prepares us to do Those Good Works

*"Jesus, <u>anointed</u> with the Holy Ghost and with power, went about doing good and healing all that were oppressed by the devil; for God was with him,"* (see Acts 10:38).

### The Anointing Destroys the Adversaries and Exalts our Horn

*"The adversaries of the Lord shall be broken to pieces; out of heaven shall he thunder upon them: the Lord shall judge the ends of the earth; and he shall give strength unto his king, and exalt the horn of his anointed,"* (1 Samuel 2:10).

## The Anointing Empowers Others

David used his anointing not only to defeat Goliath, but also to minister to everyone one that was in distress, every one that was in debt, and, every one that was discontented—about four hundred men. He turned them all into mighty men (see 1 Samuel 22:2).

The enemy of our anointing, through oppression, makes it difficult for us to walk in our liberty. It took ten plagues for Pharaoh to release the children of Israel. Until they were released, they were unable to serve God. Those of us afflicted by the fall of man have borne the image of the fallen nature; with the loss of identity, and we too, walk as mere men. But, because of the finished work of Christ, the free gift of salvation is now available to all. Having received the sufficiency of grace and the gift of righteousness, we can walk in our liberty; bearing the image, the likeness, and the dominion of the God Head.

The anointing reverses the curse and empowers us to reign over our enemies and the circumstances of life, once again. Our iniquities, our past, and the sin nature have all been reconciled to the Father by the blood of Jesus. There is now peace between God and man, and we are accepted in the beloved.

We are saved to live the predestined, preplanned, and prearranged good life ordained before the foundation of the world and to help others do the same. Being anointed, we comfort all who mourn. As we walk in our anointing we bring reconciliation to the poor, the broken hearted, the captives, the blind, and the bruised.

# The Purpose of the Anointing

The purpose of the anointing is to empower the poor, the broken hearted, the captives, the blind, and the bruised. Also, to proclaim the acceptable day of the Lord: *"To open their eyes, and to turn them from darkness to light, and from the power of Satan unto God, that they may receive forgiveness of sins, and inheritance among them which are sanctified by faith that is in me,"* (Acts 26:18).

## Preach the Gospel to the Poor

The poor are disenfranchised and stripped of their power. Due to a famine of hearing the Word of God, and keeping it, the rights of the poor have been violated. The enemy has alienated them from their rights as citizens of the kingdom of God. According to Ephesians 2:12: *"They are without Christ, being aliens from the commonwealth of Israel, and strangers from the covenant of promise."* Isaiah 42:22 (NLT) says: *"But this people have been robbed and plundered, enslaved, imprisoned, and trapped. They are fair game for anyone and have no one to protect them, no one to take them back home."* They are filled with doubt, fear, and unbelief.

Because the promises of God are foreign to the poor, they cannot access their divine nature and are therefore corrupted by the world. The enemy has robbed these individuals of their identity in Christ; they identify with their fallen nature and have become one with it. They are forgetful hearers and are snared by their own confession of lack: *"Their lips are a snare of their soul,"* says Proverbs 18:7. By not bridling their own tongue, they deceive their own hearts. Conflicted, they have difficulty dealing with the contradictions of life. They are in the field.

Being alienated from their rights, they have yielded to the spirit of anger and are easily offended; they are not able to handle the storms of life. Consider the <u>poverty</u> in the heart of the elder son as told in Luke 15: *"Now his elder son was in the field: and as he came and drew nigh to the house, he heard music and dancing. And he called one of the servants, and asked what these things meant. And he said unto him, Thy brother is come; and thy father hath killed the fatted calf, because he hath received him safe and sound.* **And he was angry, and would not go in: therefore came his father out, and intreated him.** *And he answering said to his father, Lo, these many years do I serve thee, neither transgressed I at any time thy commandment: and yet thou never gavest me a kid, that I might make merry with my friends: But as soon as this thy son was come, which hath devoured thy living with harlots, thou hast killed for him the fatted calf. And he said unto him, Son, thou art ever with me, and all that I have is thine. It was meet that we should make merry, and be glad: for this thy brother was dead, and is alive again; and was lost, and is found,"* (Luke 15:25-32). The father entreated the elder son by provoking him to love saying: *"Your bother was dead and alive again, was lost, now found,"* but, not before assuring him that he too was a son and had a right to all that was the father's.

### The Gospel (good news) for the Poor:

You are members of God's family: *"No more strangers and foreigners, but fellowcitizens with the saints, and of the household of God,"* (Ephesians 2:19).

### The Way of Escape:

*"Make no friendship with an angry man; and with a furious man thou shalt not go: Lest thou learn his ways, and get a snare to thy soul,"* (Proverbs 22:24-25).

*"But be ye doers of the word, and not hearers only, deceiving your own selves. For if any be a hearer of the word, and not a doer, he is like unto a man beholding his natural face in a glass: For he beholdeth himself, and goeth his way, and straightway forgetteth what manner of man he was. But whoso looketh into the perfect law of liberty, and continueth therein, he being not a forgetful hearer, but a doer of the work, this man shall be blessed in his deed,"* (James 1:22-25).

## Heal the Brokenhearted

The brokenhearted, through reproach (belittlement), their purposes and plans are frustrated. Their hopes and desires broken, they cry: *"Reproach hath broken my heart; and I am full of heaviness: and I looked for some to take pity, but there was none; and for comforters, but I found none,"* (Psalms 69:20).

These individuals feel that their heart's desires are broken. They believe that they are in sorrow because they are not living up to their potential; not realizing that their sorrow is due to their being yoked to unbelief. Unbelief has separated them from achieving their heart's desire. They feel forgotten, they see themselves as broken vessels. There is disquietness in their hearts. Their hedges are broken down. Their crowns have been tossed to the ground. Because of sorrow of the heart, their spirit is also broken.

The broken in heart do not realize that they have brought this waste land on themselves, because they have forsaken the Lord their God, when He tried to lead them. They did not have the fear of God and had not taken the engrafted word to save their souls: *"They, themselves, have forsaken the living water, and chose broken cisterns that could hold no water,"* (Jeremiah 2:13). They chose to walk by sight and not by faith. *"They were planted a noble vine, wholly a right seed; they were turned into a degenerate plant of a strange vine,"* (Jeremiah 2:21). They are oppressed because they walked after idols; vanity.

Consider the impotent man at the pool of Bethesda: *"And a certain man was there, which had an infirmity thirty and eight years. When Jesus saw him lie, and knew that he had been now a long time in that case, he saith unto him, Wilt thou be made whole? The impotent man answered him, Sir, I have no man, when the water is troubled, to put me into the pool: but while I am coming, another steppeth down before me. Jesus saith unto him, Rise, take up thy bed, and walk. And immediately the man was made whole, and took up his bed, and walked,"* (John 5:5-9).

For thirty-eight years this man looked for someone to take pity on him, but there was none. Walking by sight, he thought he needed to get into the pool. His unbelief, not God, was the source of his heaviness. After he separated himself from his unbelief, he arose, took up his bed, and walked.

### The Gospel (good news) for the Broken Hearted:

*"The Lord doth build up Jerusalem: he gathereth together the outcasts of Israel. He healeth the broken in heart, and bindeth up their wounds,"* (Psalms 147:2-3).

*"Therefore all they that devour thee shall be devoured; and all thine adversaries, every one of them, shall go into captivity; and they that spoil thee shall be a spoil, and all that prey upon thee will I give for a prey. For I will restore health unto thee, and I will heal thee of thy wounds, saith the Lord; because they called thee an Outcast, saying, this is Zion, whom no man seeketh after,"* (Jeremiah 30:16-17).

### The Way of Escape:

*"Take pleasure in infirmities, in reproaches, in necessities, in persecutions, in distresses for Christ's sake: for when I am weak, then am I strong,"* (2 Corinthians 12:10).

*"Come unto me, all ye that labour and are heavy laden, and I will give you rest. Take my yoke upon you, and learn of me; for I am meek and lowly in heart: and ye shall find rest unto your souls, for my yoke is easy, and my burden is light,"* (Matthew 11:28-30).

*"My righteousness I hold fast, and will not let it go: my heart shall not reproach me so long as I live,"* (Job 27: 6).

*"Having therefore these promises, dearly beloved, let us cleanse ourselves from all filthiness of the flesh and spirit, perfecting holiness in the fear of God,"* (2 Corinthians 7:1).

## Preach Deliverance to the Captive

Those in captivity, through their errors of omission, were taken captive: *"They did not destroy the nations, concerning whom the Lord commanded them: But were mingled among the heathen, and learned their works. And they served their idols: which were a snare unto them... He made them also to be pitied of all those that carried them captives,"* (Ps. 106:34-46).

These individuals were taken captive because their hearts were turned away after other gods. They lost the battle with the law in their members, which warred against the law of their minds, and they were brought into captivity to the law of sin in their members. They failed to use wisdom, they failed to forsake the foolish, and they failed to go in the way of understanding. Being simple, they did not consider the consequences. They were wise in their own eyes and prudent in their own sight. They have gone into captivity because they had no knowledge.

They were slayed because they turned away from wisdom; they wanted their own way. Through complacency they bordered on foolishness. They failed to use discernment; they believed every word. They were not crowned with knowledge; they did not foresee evil, and they passed on and were punished. By good words and fair speeches their hearts were deceived.

Consider King Solomon in 1 Kings 11. We know that he was the wisest man; given a wise and understanding heart at an early age. People traveled from far lands just to hear his wisdom. He even wrote three hundred proverbs, but the Bible says: *"But King Solomon loved many strange women... Of the nations concerning which the Lord said unto the children of Israel, Ye shall not go in to them, neither shall they come in unto you: for surely they will turn away your heart after their gods: Solomon clave unto these in love... and his heart was not perfect with the Lord his God, as was the heart of David his father. And Solomon did evil in the sight of the Lord, and went not fully after the Lord, as did David his father. And the Lord was angry with Solomon, because his heart was turned from the Lord God of Israel, which had appeared unto him twice...and had commanded him concerning this thing, that he should not go after other gods: but he kept not that which the Lord commanded. Wherefore the Lord said unto Solomon, Forasmuch as this is done of thee, and thou hast not kept my covenant and my statutes, which I have commanded thee, I will surely rend the kingdom from thee, and will give it to thy servant,"* (1 Kings 11:1-11).

God had warned King Solomon of the necessity of driving out other nations. He assured him that those that remain shall be picks in his eyes, thorns in his sides, and shall vex him in the land wherein he dwelled. His failure to drive out all the inhabitants of the land caused his heart to be turned away. He tried to serve two masters and found himself mingled, serving other gods.

### The Gospel (good news) for the Captive:

*"Shall the prey be taken from the mighty, or the lawful captive delivered? But thus saith the Lord, Even the captives of the mighty shall be taken away, and the prey of the terrible shall be delivered: for I will contend with him that contendeth with thee, and I will save thy children. And I will feed them that oppress thee with their own flesh; and they shall be drunken with their own blood, as with sweet wine: and all flesh shall know that I the Lord am thy Saviour and thy Redeemer, the mighty One of Jacob,"* (Isaiah 49:24-26).

### The Way of Escape:

*"Awake, awake; put on thy strength, O Zion; put on thy beautiful garments, O Jerusalem, the holy city: for henceforth there shall no more come into thee the uncircumcised and the unclean. Shake thyself from the dust; arise, and sit down,"* (Isaiah 52:1-2).

*"Casting down imaginations, and every high thing that exalteth itself against the knowledge of God, and bringing into captivity every thought to the obedience of Christ,"* (2 Corinthians 10:5).

## Recover the Sight of the Blind

Because of blindness, these live in error: *"They walk in the vanity of their minds; having their understanding darkened, being alienated from the life of God through the ignorance that is in them, because of the blindness of their heart: Who being past feeling have given themselves over unto lasciviousness, to work all uncleanness with greediness,"* (Ephesians 4:17-19). The blind are bowed down; they have bowed the knee to the image of Baal. They are bound by false doctrine.

These individuals, by rejecting God's statues and His covenant, chose to follow vanity and became vain. Being blinded, they walked in lack of: faith, virtue, knowledge, temperance, patience, godliness, brotherly kindness, and love; their minds blinded by the god of this world. Being ignorant of God's righteousness, they tried to establish their own. Being deceived, they trusted in vanity and received vanity as recompense. They gave lip service to the will of God; they were not steadfast in His covenant.

Now, they sit in darkness and are bound in affliction and iron, because they rebelled against the words of God, and contemned the counsel of the Most High. For the enemy has persecuted their souls; he hath made them to dwell in darkness. Their spirit is overwhelmed within them; their heart within is desolate. They come in with vanity and depart in darkness. Because they are blind, and cannot see afar off, they have forgotten that they were purged from their old sins. To prevent them from being converted, the enemy has blinded their eyes and hardened their hearts.

Consider the woman in Luke 13 who was bowed: *"Behold, there was a woman which had a spirit of infirmity eighteen years, and was bowed together, and could in no wise lift up herself. And when Jesus saw her, he called her to him, and said unto her, Woman, thou art loosed from thine infirmity. And he laid his hands on her: and immediately she was made straight, and glorified God. And the ruler of the synagogue answered with indignation, because that Jesus had healed on the sabbath day, and said unto the people, There are six days in which men ought to work: in them therefore come and be healed, and not on the sabbath day. The Lord then answered him, and said, Thou hypocrite, doth not each one of you on the sabbath loose his ox or his ass from the stall, and lead him away to watering? And ought not this woman, being a daughter of Abraham, whom Satan hath bound, lo, these eighteen years, be loosed from this bond on the sabbath day? And when he had said these things, all his adversaries were ashamed: and all the people rejoiced for all the glorious things that were done by him,"* (Luke 13:11-17).

This woman had lived in error for eighteen years, bowed down because her eyes were darkened. In Psalms 146:8, Jesus promised to open the eyes of the blind: raise them that are bowed down. Jesus was in effect saying: we water our animals, regardless of the day; she, being a daughter of Abraham, was also in need of still waters. The water of the word set her free. The blind, the ignorant, and those in darkness have bowed to false doctrines. But, *"They are sanctified and cleansed by the washing of water by the word,"* (Ephesians 5:26). Although the ruler of the synagogue was also blind, being in bondage to false doctrine and walking in the vanity of his mind, he lacked the humility to receive; he justified himself.

### The Gospel (good news) for the Blind:

*"I will bring the blind by a way that they knew not; lead them in paths that they have not known: make darkness light before them, and crooked things straight. These things they will do unto them, and not forsake them,"* (Isaiah 42:16).

### The Way of Escape:

*"Stand fast therefore in the liberty wherewith Christ hath made us free, and be not entangled again with the yoke of bondage,"* (Galatians 5:1).

## Set at Liberty the Bruised

The bruised are laden with iniquity, they show little esteem for the word of God: *"Ah sinful nation, a people laden with iniquity, a seed of evildoers, children that are corrupters: they have forsaken the Lord, they have provoked the Holy One of Israel unto anger, they are gone away backward. Why should ye be stricken anymore? ye will revolt more and more: the whole head is sick, and the whole heart faint. From the sole of the foot even unto the head there is no soundness in it; but wounds, and bruises, and putrifying sores: they have not been closed, neither bound up, neither mollified with ointment. Your country is desolate; your cities are burned with fire: your land, strangers devour it in your presence, and it is desolate, as overthrown by strangers,"* (Isaiah 1:4-8).

The bruised were corrupted by their foolishness. They have been led astray by their iniquities. Being self-willed, they sowed to the flesh and have reaped corruption. They were brought into bondage to the flesh falsely believing it would give them the liberty they were seeking. They placed their trust in things that could not profit them, while distrusting vessels of honor.

The bruised have a love affair with their flesh. They are troubled; mourning throughout the day. Their mouths pour out foolishness that perverts their way. Their hearts fret against the Lord. Their words are iniquity and deceit, and they are defiled by them. Being in the flesh, they cannot receive the things of the Spirit of God, for they are foolishness unto them. They have no spiritual discernment.

Consider the story of Achan in the book of Joshua, chapter 7. Prior to taking the city of Jericho, God told the children of Israel not to take of the spoil from Jericho because it was accursed. Achan, despising the word of God, took some of the spoil and hid it in his tent. Joshua, believing that everyone was in obedience, went on from Jericho to a little town called Ai. After engaging the battle, Israel was defeated. Bewildered, Joshua asked God what was the cause of the defeat. God answered him saying: *"Israel hath sinned, and they have also transgressed my covenant which I commanded them: for they have even taken of the accursed thing, and have also stolen, and dissembled also, and they have put it even among their own stuff. Therefore the children of Israel could not stand before their enemies, but turned their backs before their enemies, because they were accursed: neither will I be with you any more, except ye destroy the accursed from among you. Up, sanctify the people, and say, sanctify yourselves against tomorrow: for thus saith the Lord God of Israel, There is an accursed thing in the midst of thee, O Israel: thou canst not stand before thine enemies, until ye take away the accursed thing from among you. ...And it shall be, that he that is taken with the accursed thing shall be burnt with fire, he and all that he hath: because he hath transgressed the covenant of the Lord, and because he hath wrought folly in Israel,"* (Joshua 7:11-15).

God explained to Joshua that there was sin in the camp, and that the enemy could not be defeated until the rebel was dealt with. In Joshua 22:20, God called this trespass, <u>iniquity</u>. After making a diligent inquiry, Achan confessed and he and his family were stoned to death. Achan knew the word of God, but the word was not that important to him; his iniquity had more dominion over him than did the word of God. He sowed to his flesh and reaped destruction.

### The Gospel (good news) for the Bruised:
*"But he, being full of compassion, forgave their iniquity, and destroyed them not: yea, many a time turned he his anger away, and did not stir up all his wrath; For he remembered that they were but flesh; a wind that passeth away, and cometh not again,"* (Psalms 78:38-39).

### The Way of Escape:
*"He (Jesus) was oppressed, and he was afflicted, yet he opened not his mouth: he is brought as a lamb to the slaughter, and as a sheep before her shearers is dumb, so he openeth not his mouth,"* (Isaiah 53:7).

## Preach the Acceptable Year of the Lord

*"Thus saith the Lord, In an acceptable time have I heard thee, and in a day of salvation have I helped thee: and I will preserve thee, and give thee for a covenant of the people, to establish the earth, to cause to inherit the desolate heritages; That thou mayest say to the prisoners, Go forth; to them that are in darkness, Shew yourselves. They shall feed in the ways, and their pastures shall be in all high places. They shall not hunger nor thirst; neither shall the heat nor sun smite them: for he that hath mercy on them shall lead them, even by the springs of water shall he guide them. And I will make all my mountains a way, and my highways shall be exalted. Behold, these shall come from far: and, lo, these from the north and from the west; and these from the land of Sinim,"* (Isaiah 49:8-12).

**What:** *"We then, as workers together with him, beseech you also that ye receive not the grace of God in vain.*
**Why:** *(For he saith, I have heard thee in a time accepted, and in the day of salvation have I succoured thee: behold, now is the accepted time; behold, now is the day of salvation.)*
**How:** *Giving no offence in anything, that the ministry be not blamed,"* (2 Corinthians 16:1-3).

*"But in all things approving ourselves as the ministers of God, in much patience, in afflictions, in necessities, in distresses, In stripes, in imprisonments, in tumults, in labours, in watchings, in fastings; By pureness, by knowledge, by longsuffering, by kindness, by the Holy Ghost, by love unfeigned, By the word of truth, by the power of God, by the armour of righteousness on the right hand and on the left, By honour and dishonour, by evil report and good report: as deceivers, and yet true; As unknown, and yet well known; as dying, and, behold, we live; as chastened, and not killed; As sorrowful, yet alway rejoicing; as poor, yet making many rich; as having nothing, and yet possessing all things,"* (2 Corinthians 6:4-10).

142

Paul explains that the acceptable time is a grace. As ambassadors of Christ we must receive this grace and work it in our lives as an example to others so that the day of salvation, when offered, will not be without effect. When we find ourselves going from faith to doubt or from faith to fear; honoring God with our lips, but not our hearts; we are in effect, receiving the grace in vain. We are to make sure that our lives are lived in such a way as to not be a stumbling block for those in need of reconciliation.

King Saul, Israel's first king, proclaimed the acceptable time of salvation as he executed the day of vengeance against the evil report one of the tribes received, when the enemy had threaten to thrust out their right eyes: *"And told the tidings in the ears of the people: and all the people lifted up their voices, and wept. And, behold, Saul came after the herd out of the field; and Saul said, What aileth the people that they weep? And they told him the tidings of the men of Jabesh. And the Spirit of God came upon Saul when he heard those tidings, and his anger was kindled greatly. And he took a yoke of oxen, and hewed them in pieces, and sent them throughout all the coasts of Israel by the hands of messengers, saying, whosoever cometh not forth after Saul and after Samuel, so shall it be done unto his oxen. And the fear of the Lord fell on the people, and they came out with one consent. And when he numbered them in Bezek, the children of Israel were three hundred thousand, and the men of Judah thirty thousand. And they said unto the messengers that came, thus shall ye say unto the men of Jabeshgilead, Tomorrow, by that time the sun be hot, ye shall have help. And the messengers came and shewed it to the men of Jabesh; and they were glad. Therefore the men of Jabesh said, tomorrow we will come out unto you, and ye shall do with us all that seemeth good unto you. And it was so on the morrow, that Saul put the people in three companies; and they came into the midst of the host in the morning watch, and slew the Ammonites until the heat of the day: and it came to pass, that they which remained were scattered, so that two of them were not left together,"* (1 Samuel 11:4-11).

# The Anointing Disposition

In proclaiming the acceptable year of the Lord and executing the day of vengeance of our God, Saul was the first king to live the anointed lifestyle. The scripture says he was *turned into another man* and given another heart. Although he was eventually rejected as king, because he rejected the word of God, we are able to glean the principles of the disposition that brought him his ground-breaking success.

The following four landmarks (spiritual boundaries that maintain our spiritual inheritance) framed Saul's disposition; landmarks keep us within the sphere of our anointing. Saul possessed:

The Peaceful Heart: He held his peace at wickedness (see 1Samuel 10:27).
The Established Heart: He was not afraid of evil tidings (see 1 Samuel 11:5-6).
The Conquering Heart: He slew and scattered the enemy (see 1 Samuel 11:11).
The Disciplined Heart: He vexed the enemy at will (see 1 Samuel 14:47).

### Saul Holds His Peace

The children of Israel had asked God for a king. Although many were pleased with God's choice to have Saul reign as Israel's first king, some were not. The Bible calls these the children of Belial. In 1 Samuel 10:27, the Bible says: *"But the children of Belial said how shall this man save us? And they brought him no presents."* But he (Saul) held his peace.

The anointing empowers us to hold our peace. Proverbs 11:12, says: *"He that is void of wisdom despiseth his neighbor: but a man of understanding holds his peace."* For, he understands that he wrestles not against flesh and blood.

### Saul Was Not Afraid of Evil Tiding

The anointing turned Saul into another man—a man of faith. When he heard the evil tiding of the men of Jabesh, the Bible says his anger was kindled greatly. Being anointed, he operated according to Psalms 112:7-10, declaring that: *"He shall not be afraid of evil tiding: his heart is fixed trusting in the Lord. His heart is established, he shall not be afraid, until he see his desire upon his enemies... The wicked shall see it and be grieved; he shall gnash with his teeth, and melt away: the desire of the wicked shall perish."* At this time of his life, Saul's heart was fixed trusting in the Lord. He was not moved by evil tidings.

### Saul Slew and Scattered the Enemy

The Bible says in 1 Samuel 11:11 that Saul: *"Slew the Ammonites until the heat of the day: and it came to pass, that they which remained were scattered, so that two of them were not left together."*

2 Samuel describes the scattering best: *"I have pursued mine enemies, and destroyed them; and turned not again until I had consumed them,"* (2 Samuel 22:38).

### Saul Vexed the Enemy at Will

The Bible says that Saul took the kingdom of Israel and fought all his enemies on every side: *"Against Moab, against the children of Ammon, against the kings of Zobah, and against the Philistines; and whithersoever he turned himself, he vexed them,"* (1Samuel 14:47). God is saying whenever he walked in his anointing, Saul vexed them; he took captive every thought.

## The Rewards of the Anointed Life

Those who are able to live the anointed life will find that God has fortified their right hand to subdue nations. He goes before them and makes the crooked places straight and directs all of their ways. He gives them the treasures of darkness and hidden riches of secret places (see Isaiah 45:1-3).

As Saul's first assignment was to help Jabesh-Gilead, those walking in their anointing will rescue the flock and bring the exiles home.

Many of God's flock have been scattered; they are living in their foolish houses. But God assures us that there is hope in our end and that our children shall come home to their own border; for our work shall be rewarded, and they shall come again from the land of the enemy (see Jeremiah 31:16-17).

As ambassadors of Christ, we: *"Shall build the old waste places: raise up the foundations of many generations; shalt be called, The repairer of the breach, The restorer of paths to dwell in,"* (Isaiah 58:12). We are called to bear one another's burden and show them were they have erred; love edifies. We can help them to lay aside the weights and the besetting sin; then, we should empower them to bear their own burden. We should encourage them to possess the land; speaking the word only; having daily devotions, reading a chapter a day; and confessing the promises (see Appendix B).

# The Anointing Weapon

## Executing the Day of Vengeance of our God

The day of vengeance brought comfort to the mourners as was written. Isaiah 35:4-10 summarizes that day as glorious: *"Say to them that are of a fearful heart, Be strong, fear not: behold, your God will come with vengeance, even God with a recompence; he will come and save you. Then the eyes of the blind shall be opened, and the ears of the deaf shall be unstopped. Then shall the lame man leap as an hart, and the tongue of the dumb sing: for in the wilderness shall waters break out, and streams in the desert. And the parched ground shall become a pool, and the thirsty land springs of water: in the habitation of dragons, where each lay, shall be grass with reeds and rushes. And an highway shall be there, and a way, and it shall be called The way of holiness... And the ransomed of the Lord shall return, and come to Zion with songs and everlasting joy upon their heads: they shall obtain joy and gladness, and sorrow and sighing shall flee away."*

The day of vengeance executes judgment in the morning against the enemy; punishing deception: *"O house of David, thus saith the Lord; Execute judgment in the morning, and deliver him that is spoiled out of the hand of the oppressor, lest my fury go out like fire, and burn that none can quench it, because of the evil of your doings,"* (Jeremiah 21:12).

The day of vengeance requires us to command our morning — clearing our hearts from contaminating influences. *"Hast thou commanded the morning since thy days; and caused the dayspring to know his place; That it might take hold of the ends of the earth, that the wicked might be shaken out of it,"* (Job 38:12-13).

In Luke 21:22, Jesus said: *"For these be the days of vengeance, that all things which are written may be fulfilled."* Prayer, praise, and due season release the fulfillment of that which was written; ushering in the day of vengeance. **Prayer is the anointing weapon**. The type of prayer, as well as the <u>order of prayer</u>, is important.

147

## Strategic Prayers

### Prayer and praise for the midnight hour

Paul and Silas <u>prayed</u> and sang <u>praises</u> while in prison and received freedom for themselves and others: *"And at <u>midnight</u> Paul and Silas prayed, and sang praises unto God: and the prisoners heard them. And suddenly there was a great earthquake, so that the foundations of the prison were shaken: and immediately all the doors were opened, and every one's bands were loosed,"* (Acts 16:25-26).

Prayer and Praise are vital weapons of vengeance whether used alone, or together. These prayers bring the comfort as promised.

### Prayer of vow

Hannah, in bitterness of soul, vowed a vow and received a child; the petition of her prayer. *"And she vowed a vow, and said, O LORD of hosts, if thou wilt indeed look on the affliction of thine handmaid…then I will give him unto the LORD all the days of his life… For this child I prayed; and the Lord hath given me my petition which I asked of him,"* (1 Samuel 1:11-27).

### Prayer using the promises of God

Jehoshaphat prayed the written promises of God, putting Him in remembrance of His word, and received the instruction that praise was needed: *"Ye shall not need to fight in this battle: set yourselves, stand ye still, and see the salvation of the Lord with you, O Judah and Jerusalem: fear not, nor be dismayed; tomorrow go out against them: for the Lord will be with you… Jehoshaphat stood and said, Hear me, O Judah, and ye inhabitants of Jerusalem; Believe in the Lord your God, so shall ye be established; believe his prophets, so shall ye prosper. … And when they began to <u>sing and to praise</u>, the Lord set ambushments against the children of Ammon, Moab, and mount Seir, which were come against Judah; and they were smitten…and none escaped…and they were three days in gathering of the spoil, it was so much,"* (2 Chronicles 20:17-25).

## Prayers of Praise

### Praise used alone wards off destruction

*"Out of the mouth of babes and sucklings hast thou ordained strength because of thine enemies, that thou mightest <u>still the enemy and the avenger,</u>"* (Ps. 8:2).

### Praise used alone brings the presence of God

*"But thou art holy, O thou that <u>inhabitest</u> the praises of Israel,"* (Psalms 22:3).

### High praise of God to execute the written judgment

*"Let the high praises of God be in their mouth, and a two-edged sword in their hand; To execute vengeance upon the heathen, and punishments upon the people; To bind their kings with chains, and their nobles with fetters of iron; To execute upon them the judgment written: this honour have all his saints. Praise ye the Lord,"* (Psalms 149:6-9).

### Hannah's prayer of thanksgiving

*"And Hannah prayed, and said; my heart rejoiceth in the Lord, mine horn is exalted in the Lord: my mouth is enlarged over mine enemies; because I rejoice in thy salvation. There is none holy as the Lord: for there is none beside thee: neither is there any rock like our God...The adversaries of the Lord shall be broken to pieces... and exalt the horn of his anointed,"* (1 Samuel 2:1-10).

### Praise of defense and offense

*In* 2 Samuel 22:1-50, David offers a prayer of defense and offense: *"And he said, The LORD is my rock, and my fortress, and my deliverer; The God of my rock; in him will I trust: he is my shield, and the horn of my salvation, my high tower, and my refuge, my saviour; thou savest me from violence. I will call on the LORD, who is worthy to be praised: so shall I be saved from mine enemies."*

## Prayers of Faith

### Prayer to turn captivity (of unbelief, fear, and doubt)

*"And the Lord turned the captivity of Job, when <u>he prayed for his friends</u>: also the Lord gave Job twice as much as he had before,"* (Job 42:10).

### Prayer and thanksgiving brings the peace of God

*"Be careful for nothing; but in everything by prayer and supplication with thanksgiving let your requests be made known unto God. And the <u>peace of God</u>, which passeth all understanding, shall keep your hearts and minds through Christ Jesus,"* (Philippians 4:6-7).

### Prayer and fasting (unbelief) brings deliverances

*"Then Jesus answered and said, O faithless and perverse generation, how long shall I be with you? how long shall I suffer you? bring him hither to me. And Jesus rebuked the devil; and he departed out of him: and the child was cured from that very hour. Then came the disciples to Jesus apart, and said, Why could not we cast him out? And Jesus said unto them, <u>Because of your unbelief</u>: for verily I say unto you, If ye have faith as a grain of mustard seed, ye shall say unto this mountain, Remove hence to yonder place; and it shall remove; and nothing shall be impossible unto you. Howbeit this kind goeth not out but by prayer and fasting,"* (Matthew 17:17-21).

### Prayer of speaking to the problem brings mountain moving results

*"Now in the morning as he returned into the city, he hungered. And when he saw a fig tree in the way, he came to it, and found nothing thereon, but leaves only, and said unto it, Let no fruit grow on thee henceforward forever. And presently the fig tree withered away. And when the disciples saw it, they marveled, saying, How soon is the fig tree withered away! Jesus answered and said unto them, Verily I say unto you, If ye have faith, and doubt not, ye shall not only do this which is done to the fig tree, but also if ye shall say unto this*

*mountain, Be thou removed, and be thou cast into the sea; it shall be done. And all things, whatsoever ye shall ask in prayer, believing, ye shall receive,"* (Matthew 21:18-22).

### Prayer without ceasing brings angelic help/corporate prayer

*"Peter therefore was kept in prison: but prayer was made without ceasing of the church unto God for him. And when Herod would have brought him forth, the same night Peter was sleeping between two soldiers, bound with two chains: and the keepers before the door kept the prison. And, behold, the <u>angel of the Lord</u> came upon him, and a light shined in the prison: and he smote Peter on the side, and raised him up, saying, Arise up quickly. And his chains fell off from his hands,"* (Acts 12:5-7).

### Praying with all prayer

*"Finally, my brethren, be strong in the Lord, and in the power of his might; Put on the whole armour of God, that ye may be able to stand against the wiles of the devil, for we wrestle not against flesh and blood, but against principalities, against powers, against the rulers of the darkness of this world, against spiritual wickedness in high places. Wherefore take unto you the whole armour of God, that ye may be able to withstand in the evil day, and having done all, to stand. Stand therefore, having your loins girt about with truth, and having on the breastplate of righteousness; And your feet shod with the preparation of the gospel of peace; Above all, taking the shield of faith, wherewith ye shall be able to quench all the fiery darts of the wicked. And take the helmet of salvation, and the sword of the Spirit, which is the word of God: Praying always with all prayer and supplication in the Spirit, and* watching thereunto with all perseverance and supplication for all saints," (Ephesians 6:10-18).

### Prayer of commitment

*"Casting all your care upon him; for he careth for you,"* (1 Peter 5:7).

## Prayer of consecrating one's self to the will of God

*"He went away again the second time, and prayed, saying, O my Father, if this cup may not pass away from me, except I drink it, thy will be done,"* (Matthew 26:42).

*"And Mary said, Behold the handmaid of the Lord; be it unto me according to thy word. And the angel departed from her,"* (Luke 1:38).

## Prayer of faith saves the sick

*"Is any among you afflicted? let him pray. Is any merry? let him sing psalms. Is any sick among you? let him call for the elders of the church; and let them pray over him, anointing him with oil in the name of the Lord: And the prayer of faith shall save the sick, and the Lord shall raise him up; and if he have committed sins, they shall be forgiven him. Confess your faults one to another, and pray one for another, that ye may be healed. The effectual fervent prayer of a righteous man availeth much. Elias was a man subject to like passions as we are, and he prayed earnestly that it might not rain: and it rained not on the earth by the space of three years and six months. And he prayed again, and the heaven gave rain, and the earth brought forth her fruit,"* (James 5:13-18).

## Prayer in an unknown tongue to help our infirmities

*"For if I pray in an unknown tongue, my spirit prayeth, but my understanding is unfruitful. What is it then? I will pray with the spirit, and I will pray with the understanding also,"* (1 Corinthians 14:14-15).

## Prayer of binding and loosing

*"Verily I say unto you, whatsoever ye shall bind on earth shall be bound in heaven: and whatsoever ye shall loose on earth shall be loosed in heaven,"* (Matthew 18:18).

## Prayer of agreement

*"Again I say unto you, that if two of you shall agree on earth as touching anything that they shall ask, it shall be done for them of my Father which is in heaven. For where two or three are gathered together in my name, there am I in the midst of them,"* (Matthew 18:19-20).

## Ephesians prayer for wisdom

*"Cease not to give thanks for you, making mention of you in my prayers; That the God of our Lord Jesus Christ, the Father of glory, may give unto you the spirit of wisdom and revelation in the knowledge of him: The eyes of your understanding being enlightened; that ye may know what is the hope of his calling, and what the riches of the glory of his inheritance in the saints, And what is the exceeding greatness of his power to us-ward who believe, according to the working of his mighty power,"* (Ephesians 1:16-19).

*"For this cause I bow my knees unto the Father of our Lord Jesus Christ, Of whom the whole family in heaven and earth is named, That he would grant you, according to the riches of his glory, to be strengthened with might by his Spirit in the inner man; That Christ may dwell in your hearts by faith; that ye, being rooted and grounded in love, May be able to comprehend with all saints what is the breadth, and length, and depth, and height; And to know the love of Christ, which passeth knowledge, that ye might be filled with all the fulness of God. Now unto him that is able to do exceeding abundantly above all that we ask or think, according to the power that worketh in us,"* (Ephesians 3:14-20).

## The Lord's Prayer for deliverance from evil plans of enemy

*"After this manner therefore pray ye: Our Father which art in heaven, Hallowed be thy name. Thy kingdom come, thy will be done in earth, as it is in heaven. Give us this day our daily bread. And forgive us our debts, as we forgive our debtors. And lead us not into temptation, but deliver us from evil: For thine is the kingdom, and the power, and the glory, forever. Amen. For if ye forgive men their trespasses, your heavenly Father will also forgive*

you: *But if ye forgive not men their trespasses, neither will your Father forgive your trespasses,"* (Matthew 6:9-15).

## Philippians prayer for spiritual growth

*"And this I pray, that your love may abound yet more and more in knowledge and in all judgment; That ye may approve things that are excellent; that ye may be sincere and without offence till the day of Christ; Being filled with the fruits of righteousness, which are by Jesus Christ, unto the glory and praise of God,"* (Philippians 1:9-11).

## Prayer for growth in grace

*"For this cause we also, since the day we heard it, do not cease to pray for you, and to desire that ye might be filled with the knowledge of his will in all wisdom and spiritual understanding; That ye might walk worthy of the Lord unto all pleasing, being fruitful in every good work, and increasing in the knowledge of God; Strengthened with all might, according to his glorious power, unto all patience and longsuffering with joyfulness,"* (Col.1:9-11).

## Prayer of protection

*"He that dwelleth in the secret place of the most High shall abide under the shadow of the Almighty. I will say of the LORD, He is my refuge and my fortress: my God; in him will I trust. Surely he shall deliver thee from the snare of the fowler, and from the noisome pestilence. He shall cover thee with his feathers, and under his wings shalt thou trust: his truth shall be thy shield and buckler. Thou shalt not be afraid for the terror by night; nor for the arrow that flieth by day; Nor for the pestilence that walketh in darkness; nor for the destruction that wasteth at noonday. A thousand shall fall at thy side, and ten thousand at thy right hand; but it shall not come nigh thee. Only with thine eyes shalt thou behold and see the reward of the wicked. Because thou hast made the LORD, which is my refuge, even the most High, thy habitation; There shall no evil befall thee, neither shall any plague come nigh thy dwelling. For he shall give his angels charge over thee, to keep thee in all thy ways. They shall*

*bear thee up in their hands, lest thou dash thy foot against a stone. Thou shalt tread upon the lion and adder: the young lion and the dragon shalt thou trample under feet. Because he hath set his love upon me, therefore will I deliver him: I will set him on high, because he hath known my name. He shall call upon me, and I will answer him: I will be with him in trouble; I will deliver him, and honour him. With long life will I satisfy him, and shew him my salvation,"* (Psalms 91:1-16).

## Prayer Confessions

### The Blood Prayer brings reconciliation and peace

*"Now is come salvation, and strength, and the kingdom of our God, and the power of his Christ: for the accuser of our brethren is cast down, which accused them before our God day and night. And they overcame him by the blood of the Lamb and by the word of their testimony; and they loved not their lives unto the death,"* (Revelations 12:10-11).

<u>Confession:</u> we plead the bloodline of protection all around us; we place ourselves under the blood; no power of the enemy can penetrate the blood. We claim victory through the blood. We have peace through the blood; we are reconciled by the blood; cleansed by the blood; forgiven by the blood. Because we eat His flesh and drink His blood we have eternal life and He will raise us up in the last days. We have boldness to enter into the holy of holies by the blood. You passed by me and saw me polluted in my own blood you said unto me when I was I my blood, live, yea, you said unto me when I was in my blood, live! The blood of Jesus purges my conscience from dead works to serve the living God. I loose the blood of Jesus to separate me from the law of sin and death.

Confess the blood scriptures till peace comes. The blood of Jesus never fails.

## Prayer for communion:

Communion is first-aid against all attacks: physical, mental, emotional, financial, social, and spiritual. 1 Corinthians 11: 23-26, says: *"Take, eat: this is my body, which is broken for you: this do in remembrance of me. The same manner also he took the cup, when he had supped, saying, this cup is the new testament in my blood: this do ye, as oft as ye drink it, in remembrance of me. For as often as ye eat this bread, and drink this cup, ye do shew the Lord's death till he come."* Take as often: daily, morning and evening, upon an attack, or as the Lord leads.

<u>Communion confession</u>: Mountains moved out of my life, battles won without having to fight, I miss the mess, deliverance from fear, reverse the curse, and release the covenant promises of God into my life.

## Releasing angels, ministering spirits

*"But to which of the angels said he at any time, Sit on my right hand, until I make thine enemies thy footstool? Are they not all ministering spirits, sent forth to minister for them who shall be heirs of salvation,"* (Hebrews 1:13-14).

*"Bless the Lord, ye his angels that excel in strength, that do his commandments, hearkening unto the voice of his word,"* (Psalms 103:20).
<u>Confession</u>: Angels go, go ministering spirits, and cause our blessings to come, in Jesus' name.

## Prayer confession to move mountains

<u>Confession</u>: Mountain, be removed and be cast into the sea. I doubt not in my heart, but I believe those things I say shall come to pass and I can have whatsoever I say.

Who are thou, O great mountain, thou shall become a plain. I bring the head cornerstone thereof to it crying: grace, grace unto it in Jesus' name and I believe I receive it, in Jesus' name. Amen

### Prayer confession to communicate your faith

*"I have faith that subdued kingdoms, wrought righteousness, obtained promises, stopped the mouths of lions, Quenched the violence of fire, escaped the edge of the sword, out of weakness were made strong, waxed valiant in fight, turned to flight the armies of the aliens,"* (Hebrews 11:33-34).

## A Better Resurrection

When it appears that your prayers are not answered, stay in faith. God is preparing a better resurrection for you. Hebrews 11:35, says: *"Women received their dead raised to life again: and others were tortured, not accepting deliverance; that they might obtain a better resurrection."* A better resurrection is a principle. If you stay in faith, God will give you what you asked for, or better. Jesus, in the garden of Gethsemane, asked if the cup could pass from Him. God couldn't give him that desire, but He gave Him a better desire: a better resurrection (see Mathew 26:42; Matthews 28:6).

## Can You Watch One Hour?

**Power released from one-hour prayer watch:**
- The soul is restored. (Matthew 26:40-41; Psalms 23:3)
- The city (flesh) is made desolate. (Revelation 18:19)
- (Enemy's) Judgment is come. (Revelation 18:10)
- Riches (wisdom) of the enemy come to nought. (Revelation 18:17)
- Praying in the spirit separates you from the flesh and ministers healing. (Romans 8:26)

**Effective one-hour prayer to include:**
- Blood Prayer: Revelations 12:11
- Dominion Prayer: Colossians 2:15
- Speaking to the mountain: Mark 11:23-24
- Calling those things that be not as though they were: Romans 4:17 (I call my body healed, recovered; I call all attacks stayed and cast into the sea, I believe I receive it in Jesus' Name).
- Sanctify yourself: curse confusion and loose the wisdom of God.
- High praise and thanksgiving: Psalms 144-150

## Using Your Faith

When I got a skin irritation, I was accustomed to going to the store and applying some hydrocortisone cream, until one day the Holy Spirit told me to: "Use your faith."

I began speaking to the attack, believing I received it and calling all attacks stayed and cast into the sea. Soon without the use of medicine, the rash was gone. Later, I realized that I was not healed when my skin healed; I was healed two thousand years ago when Jesus went to the cross and bought my healing as one of my benefit packages. Since that time, the Holy Spirit has taken me back to Psalms 103 to remind me that when He saved me, He also healed me. In other words, symptoms do not mean that you are not healed.

From time to time, I have had to stand for the manifestation of my healing. One word of comfort I recently found is that we must build a defense against the attack until it is subdued (see Deuteronomy 20:20). The New Testament calls this due season (see Galatians 6:9). Healing is sometimes a process: first the blade, then the corn, and after that the full corn in the ear.

In contending for the faith: Psalm 103 1:1-5 says to: *"Bless the Lord, O my soul: and all that is within me, bless his holy name. Bless the Lord, O my soul, and forget not all his <u>benefits:</u> Who forgiveth all thine iniquities; who healeth all thy diseases; who redeemeth thy life from destruction..."* God is saying that your healing is a given, now use your <u>importunity</u> till due season.

Isaiah 53:4-5 says: *"<u>Surely</u> he hath borne our griefs, and carried our sorrows: yet we did esteem him stricken, smitten of God, and afflicted. But he was wounded for our transgressions; he was bruised for our iniquities: the chastisement of our peace was upon him; and with his stripes we are healed."* I have heard it said: sometimes God heals slowly, sometimes fast, but it's always <u>surely</u>. Fighting the good fight of faith will require despising the shame, and enduring till the end.

# Epilogue

Thoughts are the forerunners of life and death; they define our existence and act as governors directing us toward particular paths of life. An unexamined life may never suspect that it was an unchallenged thought or frame of reference lying at the helm of a poor decision.

Once a thought is received, it's only a matter of time before it's acted on. Knowing the significance of our thoughts, God gave us His Word so that we could know His thoughts. God-like thoughts always place us in the spirit, where we can exercise dominion over the adverse circumstances of life.

The story of Gedaliah is an example of what can happen when thoughts from the flesh are not resisted. Eat and drink, the flesh says, but his heart is not with us. In other words, think it, speak it, and don't guard your mouth.

No, we must consider what we think and speak; then, what we eat and drink; as thoughts are not made in isolation.

The content of this book is tantamount to **spying out the land.** As you continue to explore the Word of God, I pray that the Holy Spirit will empower you to occupy until He comes—take the land that's yours and possess it. Begin with the fruit of the Spirit; for that's your treasure, the secret of your strength.

## Salvation Prayer

Father, I come to you in the name of Jesus. I believe that Jesus died for my sins. I believe that He was raised from the dead for my justification. Jesus, come into my heart, and take over my life; be my Lord and my Savior. I believe I receive you. Now, I am saved in Jesus name, Amen. Welcome to the household of faith.

# Appendix A

## Types of Flesh in the Bible

### OT Books

| GENESIS | The tree of the knowledge of good and evil |
|---|---|
| EXODUS | Taskmaster |
| LEVITICUS | Strange fire; sin of ignorance |
| NUMBERS | Balaam |
| DEUTERONOMY | Giants (in the land); the tail |
| JOSHUA | Jordan ( overflows it banks all the times of harvest); accursed thing |
| JUDGES | Midianites |
| RUTH | First kinsman |
| 1 SAMUEL | Goliath; Penninnah |
| 2 SAMUEL | Amalekites |
| 1 KINGS | Solomon's strange wives |
| 2 KINGS | Jezebel |
| 1 CHRONICLES | Michal the daughter of Saul, despising king David's dance |
| 2 CHRONICLES | Young men counsel to Rehoboam |
| EZRA | Hired counsellors to frustrate their purpose |
| NEHEMIAH | Enemy in the Midst (To cause the work to cease) |
| ESTHER | Wicked Haman |
| JOB | Miserable Comforter; (Accuser of the brethren) |
| PSALMS | Strange children; the foolish; the wicked; the scorner; the ungodly; the rebel; flattering lips; lying lips; deceitful tongue |
| PROVERBS | Rule; the simple; perverse lips; the froward; the net; wood |

# Appendix A
## Types of Flesh in the Bible

### OT Books

| | |
|---|---|
| ECCLESIASTES | *Vanity; folly; babbler* |
| SONG OF SOLOMAN | *Little foxes that spoil the vine* |
| ISAIAH | *Sinful nation; the blind; the prophet that teaches lies; he is the tail* |
| JEREMIAH | *Fallow ground; thorns* |
| LAMENTATIONS | *Her prophets; her priests* |
| EZEKIEL | *Impudent children; stiff hearted; rebellious house; bloody city* |
| DANIEL | *fiery furnace* |
| HOSEA | *Inhabitants of the land; idols; deceitful bow* |
| JOEL | *Valley of decision* |
| AMOS | *Judge in the midst; polluted land; waste cities* |
| OBADIAH | *Pride of thy heart* |
| JONAH | *Big fish* |
| MICAH | *Incurable wound; polluted rest; seers; diviners; Babylon; thy own house; darkness* |
| NAHUM | *Bloody city; wicked counsellor* |
| HABAKKUK | *Bitter and hasty nation; the proud man* |
| ZEPHANIAH | *Oppressing city; rejoicing city that dwelt carelessly* |
| HAGGAI | *Former house; drought; unclean* |
| ZECHRIAH | *Adamant stone heart* |
| MALACHI | *Impoverished* |

# Appendix A

## Types of Flesh in the Bible

NT Books

| MATTHEW | *False prophet in sheep's clothing; corrupt tree; foolish man; Pharisees; goats; the field; sand* |
|---------|---------------------------------------------------------------------------------------------------|
| MARK | *From within proceeds evil; tradition of elders; faithless generation; scribes; hard heart; stony ground; thorny ground; fig tree* |
| LUKE | *Far country; beam in eye; man without a foundation; unbelievers* |
| JOHN | *Hireling; robbers* |
| ACTS | *Mean city; full of subtilty; mischief; enemy of all righteousness; pervert right way of the Lord* |
| ROMANS | *Condemnation; wretched man; body of death* |
| 1 CORINTHIANS | *Carnal* |
| 2 CORINTHIANS | *Every high thing that exalts itself against the knowledge of God; letter kills; minds blinded* |
| GALATIANS | *False Brethren; law, school master; dissimulation; bondwomen* |
| EPHESIANS | *Corrupt communication* |
| PHILIPPIANS | *Crooked and perverse nation* |
| COLOSIANS | *Man who beguiles with enticing words; man who spoils through philosophy and vain deceit* |
| 1 THESSALONIANS | *Unruly; lust of concupiscence* |

# Appendix A

## Types of Flesh in the Bible

| 2 THESSALONIANS | Soon shaken in mind; unreasonable and wicked men |
|---|---|
| 1 TIMOTHY | Vain jangling; contrary to sound doctrine |
| 2 TIMOTHY | Hardness; profane; vain babbling; ungodliness; vessel of wood; youthful lusts; lovers of self; loves of pleasures; disobedient to parents; unthankful; unholy; itching ears; etc. |
| TITUS | Vain talkers; subvert whole houses; liars; foolish questions; heretic |
| PHILEMON | Unprofitable servant |
| HEBREWS | Strange country |
| JAMES | Double minded; tongue full of deadly poison; unruly evil; lust that wars in our members, the rich man |
| 1 PETER | Vain conversation; the proud |
| 2 PETER | As natural brute beast; cunningly devised tales; servant of corruption; presumptuous; self-willed |
| 1 JOHN | Lust of eyes; lust of flesh; pride of life; hate the brethren |
| 2 JOHN | Deceivers |
| 3 JOHN | Love preeminence |
| JUDE | Lasciviousness; murmurs; complainers; mockers; speak evil of things they know not |
| REVELATION | Neither hot nor cold; left first love; seduce servant to fornication; wretched; miserable; poor; blind and naked |

# Appendix B

## Confessions

*Confess the following until peace comes:*

| | |
|---|---|
| DOMINION | And having spoiled principalities and powers, he made a shew of them openly, triumphing over them in it. (Colossians 2:15 ) |
| DOMINION | The Lord shall cause thine enemies that rise up against thee to be smitten before thy face: they shall come out against thee one way, and flee before thee seven ways. (Deuteronomy 28:7) |
| DOMINION | Behold, I give unto you power to tread on serpents and scorpions, and over all the power of the enemy: and nothing shall by any means hurt you. (Luke 10:19) |
| DOMINION | No weapon that is formed against thee shall prosper; and every tongue *that* shall rise against thee in judgment thou shalt condemn. This *is* the heritage of the servants of the Lord, and their righteousness *is* of me, saith the Lord. (Isaiah 54:17) |
| DOMINION | Forasmuch then as the children are partakers of flesh and blood, he also himself likewise took part of the same; that through death he might destroy him that had the power of death, that is, the devil; And deliver them who through fear of death were all their lifetime subject to bondage. (Hebrews 2:14-15) |
| DOMINION | Ye are of God, little children, and have overcome them: because greater is he that is in you, than he that is in the world. (1 John 4:4) |
| DOMINION | Now thanks be unto God, which always causeth us to triumph in Christ... (2 Corinthians 2:14) |
| DOMINION | But thanks *be* to God, which giveth us the victory through our Lord Jesus Christ. (1 Corinthians 15:57) |
| HEALTH | Surely he hath borne our griefs, and carried our sorrows: yet we did esteem him stricken, smitten of God, and afflicted. But he *was* wounded for our transgressions; *he was* bruised for our iniquities: the chastisement of our peace *was* upon him; and with his stripes we are healed. (Isaiah 53:4-5) |

# Appendix B

## Confessions

*Confess the following until peace comes*

| | |
|---|---|
| HEALTH | For the law of the Spirit of life in Christ Jesus hath made me free from the law of sin and death. (Romans 8:2) |
| HEALTH | My eye is not dim, nor natural force abated. (Deuteronomy 34: 7) |
| HEALTH | Bless the Lord, O my soul: and all that is within me *bless* his holy name. Bless the Lord, O my soul, and forget not all his benefits: Who forgiveth all thine iniquities; who healeth all thy diseases; Who redeemeth thy life from destruction; who crowneth thee with lovingkindness and tender mercies; Who satisfieth thy mouth with good *things; so that* thy youth is renewed like the eagle's. (Psalms 103:1-5) |
| HEALTH | The memory of the just *is* blessed: but the name of the wicked shall rot. (Proverbs 10:7) |
| HEALTH | The thoughts of the righteous *are* right: *but* the counsels of the wicked *are* deceit. (Proverbs 12:5) |
| FAITH | For whatsoever is born of God overcometh the world: and this is the victory that overcometh the world, *even* our faith. (1 John 5:4) *I have world overcoming faith.* |
| FAITH | But ye, beloved, building up yourselves on your most holy faith, praying in the Holy Ghost, Keep yourselves in the love of God, ... (Jude 1:20-21) |
| FAITH | I have faith that: subdued kingdoms, wrought righteousness, obtained promises, stopped the mouths of lions, Quenched the violence of fire, escaped the edge of the sword, out of weakness were made strong, waxed valiant in fight, turned to flight the armies of the aliens. (Hebrews 11:33-34) |
| FAITH | I am crucified with Christ: nevertheless I live; yet not I, but Christ liveth in me: and the life which I now live in the flesh I live by the faith of the Son of God, who loved me, and gave himself for me. (Galatians 2:20) |
| FEAR | There is no fear in love; but perfect love casteth out fear: because fear hath torment. He that feareth is not made perfect in love. (1 John 4:18) |
| FEAR | For God hath not given us the spirit of fear; but of power, and of love, and of a sound mind. (2 Timothy 1:7) |

# Appendix B

## Confessions

*Confess the following until peace comes:*

| | |
|---|---|
| FEAR | Let us therefore fear, lest, a promise being left us of entering into his rest, any of you should seem to come short of it. (Hebrews 4:1) |
| FEAR | Fear ye not, stand still, and see the salvation of the Lord, which he will shew to you today: for the Egyptians whom ye have seen today, ye shall see them again no more forever.  The Lord shall fight for you, and ye shall hold your peace. (Ex 14:13-14) |
| FEAR | This day will I begin to put the dread of thee and the fear of thee upon the nations *that are* under the whole heaven, who shall hear report of thee, and shall tremble, and be in anguish because of thee. (Deuteronomy 2:25) |
| FEAR | The fear of man bringeth a snare: but whoso putteth his trust in the Lord shall be safe. (Proverbs 29:25) |
| EMPOWERMENT | I can do all things through Christ which strengthened me. (Philippians 4:13) |
| EMPOWERMENT | Nay, in all these things we are more than conquerors through him that loved us, (Romans 8:37) |
| COMFORT | Who hath delivered us from the power of darkness, and hath translated *us* into the kingdom of his dear Son. (Colossians 1:13) |
| CONFUSION | There are many devices in a man's heart; nevertheless the counsel of the Lord, that shall stand. (Proverbs 19:21) |
| PEACE | Great peace have they which love thy law: and nothing shall offend them. (Psalms 119:165) |
| PEACE | Thou wilt keep *him* in perfect peace, *whose* mind *is* stayed *on thee*: because he trusteth in thee. (Isaiah 26:3) |
| BLOOD | And they overcame him by the blood of the Lamb, and by the word of their testimony; and they loved not their lives unto the death. (Revelation 12:11) |

# Appendix B

## Confessions

*Confess the following until peace comes:*

| | |
|---|---|
| SELF-ESTEEM | I will praise thee; for I am fearfully *and* wonderfully made: marvellous *are* thy works; and *that* my soul knoweth right well. (Psalms 139:14) |
| PROMISED REST | Blessed *be* the Lord, that hath given rest unto his people Israel, according to all that he promised: there hath not failed one word of all his good promise, which he promised by the hand of Moses his servant. (1 Kings 8:56) |
| FINANCE | But my God shall supply all your need according to his riches in glory by Christ Jesus. (Philippians 4:19) |
| CHARACTER OF GOD | God *is* not a man, that he should lie; neither the son of man, that he should repent: hath he said, and shall he not do *it*? or hath he spoken, and shall he not make it good? Behold, I have received *commandment* to bless: and he hath blessed; and I cannot reverse it. (Numbers 23:19-20) |
| BLESSING | God turned the curse into a blessing unto thee, because the Lord thy God loved thee. (Deuteronomy 23:5) |
| FAVOUR | Thou shalt arise, *and* have mercy upon Zion: for the time to favour her, yea, the set time, is come (Psalms 102:13) |
| PROMISE | So shall my word be that goeth forth out of my mouth: it shall not return unto me void, but it shall accomplish that which I please, and it shall prosper *in the thing* whereto I sent it. (Isaiah 55:11-12) |
| COVENANT OF PEACE | For the mountains shall depart, and the hills be removed; but my kindness shall not depart from thee, neither shall the covenant of my peace be removed, saith the Lord that hath mercy on thee. (Isaiah 54:10) |
| ESTABLISHED HEART | He shall not be afraid of evil tidings: his heart is fixed, trusting in the Lord. His heart *is* established, he shall not be afraid, until he see *his desire* upon his enemies. (Psalms 112:7-8) |
| DOMINION | The wicked shall see *it*, and be grieved; he shall gnash with his teeth, and melt away: the desire of the wicked shall perish. (Psalms 112:10) |
| DOMINION | And they shall fight against thee; but they shall not prevail against thee; for I *am* with thee, saith the Lord, to deliver thee. (Jeremiah 1:19) |

```
                    ┌─────────────────────┐
                    │     Love God        │
                    │  (Deuteronomy 6:5)  │
                    │                     │
        ┌───────────┼─────────────────────┼───────────────────┐
        │   Love    │                     │  Love Thy Neighbor │
        │  Yourself │   THE LOVE TEST     │   (Romans 13:9)    │
        │(Matthew   │                     │                    │
        │  22:39)   │                     │                    │
        └───────────┼─────────────────────┼───────────────────┘
                    │                     │
                    │                     │
                    │  Love Your Enemies  │
                    │   (Matthew 5:44)    │
                    └─────────────────────┘
```

This test focuses on the presence of the "Love Walk" in your life. We are called to love God, love our neighbor as ourselves, love our enemies, and love the unthankful; owe no man anything, but love. When you pass the "Love Test", you have entered into a state of maturity.

Carolyn Chambers

|  | No answer?<br>Go again 7 times<br>(1 Kings 18:43) |  |
|---|---|---|
| Go from<br>Faith to Faith<br>(Romans 1:17) | **THE FAITH TEST** | When Moses hands were up, he prevailed<br>(Exodus 17:11) |
|  | Joshua withdrew not back his hands till all inhabitants were destroyed<br>(Joshua 8:26) |  |

We are commanded to build a defense, when we are attacked, until the enemy is subdued. We are to endure till due season. It calls for us to go from one confession of faith to the next confession of faith; do not withdraw until all enemies of our soul are destroyed; keep a watch and go again until we win.

170

**Doubt**

I doubt not in my heart

(Mark 11:23)

**Fear**

Perfect love cast out fear
(1 John 4:18)

**THE PRIDE TEST**

**Unbelief**

I stagger not at the promises of God through unbelief (Romans 4:20)

**Presumption**

Keep back thy servant from presumptuous sins

(Psalms 19:13)

Wisdom is the antidote for pride. When the light of God's word shines in the darkness, the darkness cannot apprehend it; it has no defense against the Word of God. We are called to guard against: fear, doubt, and unbelief, which lead to presumptuous actions. This is accomplished as we retain God in all our thoughts.

Set my face like a
flint, I shall not be
ashamed

(Isaiah 50:7)

Despising the shame

(Hebrews 12:2)

**THE SHAME
TEST**

In nothing shall I be
ashamed

(Philippians 5:12)

Hope makes me
not ashamed

(Romans 5:5)

For our shame we shall possess the double; we shall have praise and fame where we have been put to shame. We are called to despise the shame: to see it as little or nothing at all; set our face like a flint; in nothing shall we be ashamed and whosoever believes on Him shall not be put to shame.

*BLESSED ARE THEY THAT DO HIS COMMANDMENTS,*

*THAT THEY MAY HAVE RIGHT TO*

*THE TREE OF LIFE*

*AND MAY ENTER IN*

*THROUGH THE GATES INTO THE CITY*

REVELATIONS 22:14

# Also from Anointed Life Publishing:

### DISCOVERING YOUR ANOINTING NUMBERS
By Carolyn Chambers

In her life-changing new book, Carolyn Chambers helps readers discover their anointing numbers and empowers them to fight life's great battle-themselves. Simply put—everyone is at war with themselves. But, walking anointed is something everyone can achieve. In, "Discovering Your Anointing Numbers: Allow me to introduce you to Yourself," Carolyn Chambers examines the influence that birth demographics have on human behavior. This is a compelling read for all.

### SKI: MEMOIRS OF A VIETNAM VET
By Al Sutton

The war did not end for Ralph. It resumes on even the slightest provocation: A tree line on a freeway instantly becomes a place where enemy fire erupts from, and rain brings back vivid memories of the horrors of war in the jungles of Vietnam. In both prose and haunting poetry, we follow Ralph on a fascinating journey of war with first-hand accounts of battles at the height of the Vietnam War, and a thriller inner-battle that awaited him, on the home front. Despite the odds, Ralph discovers a more powerful weapon that will defeat all of his enemies and change his life forever.

## We invite you to visit our website at:
## Anointed Life Publishing

## www.anointedlifepublishing.com

To get information regarding having the author speak to your group, organization, or church, please email us at: carolyn.allow@yahoo.com

CPSIA information can be obtained at www.ICGtesting.com
Printed in the USA
BVOW07s1816220814

363873BV00001B/7/P